Harsh Reality, ImPossible Dream

A Memoir of Hard Times, Better Times, and the Best Times

By
Shanise F. Craft

ISBN 978-1-61658-812-0

First I would like to say that without God's grace and mercy over my life I don't know where I would be.

I would like to dedicate this book to my mother, Barbara, to my four beautiful children, Tiffanie, Brittney, Amber, and Jesurun. We have all walked through the fire together and hit the bottom. Through God's continued grace, mercy and favor we can only go up from here and will always be there for one another.

Amber, Britt, Jesurun, and Tiff—my inspirations.

Washington Heights on Sugar Hill in the heart of New York City. When I was a child growing into a young mother and a woman, no one ever taught me how to personally manage myself. I had on-the-job hands-on training which helped me to become the businesswoman I am today. I knew how to manage a line of credit for a company that covered millions of dollars in inventory and business credit floorplans.

What I didn't know was life outside of work, how to cut a person off from me, how to say NO, and how to move on. People will go as far as you allow them to. Throughout this book you will see how I chose to ignore many of the signs I received. Countless times I had the feeling that things were not always right. Unfortunately, I learned the hard way that nine out of ten times ignoring those feelings led me into a not-so-good situation.

Although I tried to be a good, supportive, giving person and because of my heart for God I was always wanting to help, my kindness has more often been taken for a weakness. The biggest lesson I learned is when a person is a user they will get all there is to get from you and when you don't have any more to give they will move on to someone else. There is no loyalty when it comes to a person with a using, get-over spirit.

God humbled me. He gave me chance after chance until he finally became fed up and told me, "Young lady, enough is enough!" God commanded my attention, and therefore, at that very moment he took it. He humbled me by taking many things out of my life. I lost a lot of material things because I was not a good steward over my money.

Proverbs 13:22: The wealth of the sinner is stored up for the righteous. It was not meant to be the other way around. I spent money on and gave money to people that God never intended me to. He made this clear to me. This year, going into my new season, "I get it." I had to prove to God that my loyalty will be to him. I now pray before, not after, I make a decision. Important as it is, I have now learned and understand how to walk away. Be careful and make sure the person you would give your last dime to is really worthy of it.

I pray that you are blessed through the trials of my life.

Shanise

"If you give yourself to the hungry and satisfy the desire of the afflicted, then your light will rise in darkness and your gloom will become like midday. And the LORD will continually guide you … you will be like a watered garden, and like a spring of water whose waters do not fail."
Isaiah 58:10-11 NASB

I start and end every day with prayer, thanking God every morning and every night regardless of what the day brings. I let my father know that I appreciate what he has allowed me to have and I appreciate his seeing fit to use me to help spread his word. Although the following list may seem extremely long, I'm sure that after reading how far I've come, you will understand. I am grateful and have to give thanks to everyone he has placed in my path, all of whom have made this book possible.

My four beautiful children, Tiffanie, Brittney, Amber, and Jesurun, I love you all so much and thank you for being such amazing, understanding, caring, supportive children; you are my true inspirations. My awesome mother, Barbara Singleton, you did a great job raising me. I learned how to be a strong, independent woman from you. I love you so very much. Thank you for all your sacrifices. Aunt Ann Deans, I appreciate the times you gave up your leisure time just so that you could babysit me. You have been a role model, a great friend, and have always played a major role in my life. My uncle Anthony Singleton, I know you have always said you didn't have much to give, but Uncle, you gave me all you had. I love you, and I admire the way you stepped up to the call and became the man of the family without hesitation. DySheka and Jasmine Deans, I love you, Cousins. Thanks for supporting us and showing up at both my and the kids' special moments. My twin brothers, Craig and Gregory Pearce, I am so happy to call you my brothers. I love you guys. My brother, Willie V. Craft, thanks for walking down a different path; you are a wonderful father to your children. To my other child, Shavonna Rodriguez, I miss you, and to my sister in Christ Darlene Hatcher, from one single mother to another, you've done such a great job with her; I am so proud of the young woman Shavonna has blossomed into. Uncle Gearni "G-Money" Thompson, I love you and I want to thank you for exposing me to the world of entertainment and having my back with marketing/promotions. Special thanks to my aunts Gloria Jones, Elaine Singleton, Sheila Singleton, and to my great-aunt Harriet Simmons and her brother, my great-uncle Banov Simmons. Thank you to all of my family, far too many to name, but I love you all, aunts, uncles, nephews, and cousins.

Mrs. Sheila Stewart Russell of the *Russ Parr Morning Show* on WKYS 93.9 FM. You have inspired me to soar to the highest level. Thank you for always being you. Pastor Bill Russell of the International Worship Center, you are such an awesome man of God. I thank you for your pure heart, and I love you. My best friend, Cheryl Giles, I love you and have to say thank you for all your prayers and encouragement. We cried and laughed together, but thank you for keeping your boxing gloves on and not letting me get discouraged or give up. Thank you for the discernment and for protecting me by bringing to my attention the things in my life that shouldn't be. Rebecca Richardson, I love you and appreciate you. I will be here every step of the way with you. Mrs. Alma Brown— she's my Gayle and I'm her Oprah.

Special thanks and appreciation to my bishops, a truly godly husband-and-wife team who have done so much for my family—I love them very much—and to Pastor Earline Payne for keeping my family lifted in prayer. To National Chair of the National Congress of Black Women Dr. E. Faye Williams, Esq.; my friend and encourager jazz great Kenny Carr (Tigers), who always knew the right things to say to me just when I needed to hear them. Special thanks to rap legend Doug E. Fresh. Special thanks to Nicole Kirby. Special thanks to the Fox 5 DC family, Michelene Bowman, Wisdom Martin, Roz Plater, and news anchor Allison Seymour. Thanks to Pastor Matt Anderson and his lovely wife Kem of Grace and Truth Bible Church, Pastor Dr. Jamal Bryant of Empowerment Temple Church, and to my daughter Tiffanie's church-covering Pastors Drs. Mike and DeeDee Freeman of Spirit of Faith Christian Center (you have made an impact on her life). Bobby Burwell of

Praise 104.1 FM. Thank you to motivational speaker Dr. Lonise Bias (mother of the late great basketball star Len Bias), Dr. Charlene Dukes (president of Prince George's Community College), Alvin Waples of Majic 102.3 FM, Denise Rolark Barnes of *The Washington Informer*, and editor Sarah Andrews (Sundragon Editing). A very special thank you to Bishop Wiley Jackson and First Lady Mary Jackson of Gospel Tabernacle (Atlanta, GA) "Word In Action" for opening the doors to my worship.

And thanks to that group of friends who saw the vision and became excited about where God was taking me, anticipating seeing my dreams come true, especially the dealership coming to pass: DR Cunningham, Ashley Logan, Janet Cooksey, Carissa Munns, Ernest and Darienne Merchant (frugalyetfly.com), Lisa Ennis (eccentrics-spa.com), Arndrea Jackson, Holeeta Cain (holeeta@gmail.com), Gerald Evans (on facebook), Deunka Wade (cuteface@comcast.net), Angelo Collington, Elliot Lyles and John Fitzgerald Booty (retired NFL).

Contents

Introduction

God Protects Babies and Fools:
The Older Generation Would Say You Had the Wool Pulled over Your Eyes,
I Say Now It's Silk

It's hard to know where to start this book, so many things have happened to me throughout my life. Instead of opening with one special memory, I would like to start by saying yes, it is true, God takes care of babies and fools. You'll figure out which one I was as you read along. I wrote down these memories as they came to me, and they didn't always come to me in order, so instead of this being your normal book written with straight narrative in chronological order, let's think of this as my open diary. I will need you to follow along with me through some twists and turns.

I have to give God all the glory and honor for allowing me to be sitting here telling my story. I wasn't sure how to do it or what to write; I only knew that I wanted my words and my story to help other single mothers out there. Being a single mother, actually being a single parent, whether you're a mother or a father, does not come easy. Most people do not realize that when you become a parent your life is not yours until the eighteen-year commitment is fulfilled, and if your kids go off to college you can add an additional four years to that. I watched my mother raise me on her own and never realized how hard it was until I became a mommy myself. In my adult life, I've seen prosperity and bankruptcy, I've watched one of my children battle a mysterious illness, I've experienced a couple of bad relationships, and I've been surprised by the number of people who hear a little bit of my story and tell me they're hungry to hear more.

After praying and really thinking for a while, I realized I just have to tell my story. When you read this you will hear the truth as I recall it, and it's not going to be all glamour either. I will tell you all about what I have walked through and seen on my paths as a single mother and an African American female running a luxury car dealership in the state of Maryland. As I was writing the book with all the memories coming up, I cried through some chapters, laughed through others, and I had a lot of Steve Urkel moments: "Did I Do That!?" Often I became mad at myself and just had to pray and continue writing. My prayers are that my story might help young women and young men to notice the signs and catch on to the things that aren't as they appear, things that I myself just didn't see, though they were staring me right in the face. I pray that my story will help a young woman or a young man to head in a different direction and not make the same mistakes I did.

You will hear all about the sex, lies, and drugs, and about my being in the boys' club of the car industry. Most importantly, you will see how, although I wasn't baptized until October 4, 1998, when I was an adult with children of my own, God had his hand on my life all along. I may not have realized it at the time, but God covered me, he had a plan for me, and I believe this book you're reading right now is part of that plan.

You see, I went astray for a while, I had fallen and given in to lust, but I was scared straight by God. As Donnie McClurkin would say, "We fall down but get back up." I slipped out of grace and had to rededicate my life to God. I have been single and in line with God since October 18, 2006. That date marks the last day I was going to sleep with a man and take myself out of the will of God. That moment of intimacy was one of the worst moments in my life. It was horrible. God made sure I was going to remember that day. The man reeked of cigarettes, and I am not a smoker—it was awful. I decided that day that I would not get into another relationship until I found something that could be blessed by God.

Chapter 1

Beginnings

～

It's springtime. I was born in New York in May 1970, to Sylvester and Barbara. When I was around three months old, my mother was arrested for stabbing my father because not only did he get caught cheating on her with my now stepmother Sharon, he tried to deny that I was his child, listening to his mother along with trying to put on the big bad act. I recently spoke with my mother about the details surrounding the incident. It seems my godfather Ike did not like Sharon, so he went and told my mother that my father was cheating on her and the lady and her daughter were both at my grandmother's house that very moment. My mother went over to my grandmother Louise's house, and there was my dad sitting at the kitchen table with Sharon and her daughter. When my mother saw this, she went into a rage. My dad and grandmother tried to talk to her; the three of them went outside the apartment into the hallway of the building. My mother had placed a knife underneath my baby carrier on her way over to the apartment; in her mind, had they tried anything to harm her, she was going to cut the two of them—my father and Sharon. Fortunately for Sharon, since she stayed inside the apartment my mother couldn't get to her. My dad was not so lucky; my mom stabbed him, then grabbed me and left. Sharon had to help him—screaming and hollering, with blood dripping down—into the car to drive him to the hospital with the knife still sticking out of his arm. Because of the knife and the actual assault, the hospital, following protocol, had to report the incident to the police. Nearly two weeks went by before they came to arrest my mother. Lucky for her, my dad did not press charges. The two of them were ordered to counseling, and in the end my dad was ordered to pay child support and he and my mom went their separate ways. He declined to take a paternity test because he knew I was his daughter, regardless of what his very own mother had said. I ended up with his last name. Sad to say, I never had a relationship with his mother and my grandmother Louise. She would see me in the street—a few times I said hello to her and she would just keep on walking, never would even acknowledge me. I was okay with that because ninety-five percent of those times I saw her drunk walking through the streets. I honestly do not feel like I missed out on anything, and seeing her act that way showed me who had taught my dad his mean and nasty ways.

I applaud my mother; she raised me alone and took care of me and didn't take any stuff from my father. Mr. Craft had finally met his match in a woman that wouldn't take any mess from him and wouldn't let him run over her, which of course led to a quick breakup. My mother was not a weak woman, she was not insecure, and she was not dependant on a man. My dad wouldn't even visit me at the front door because of that very thing; I would always have to meet him around the corner. My mother was the strong woman I wanted to grow up to be.

My life was strange growing up, and I never understood what my mother's thoughts were. I only wished one thing of her, and that was an understanding of why we lived separate from my brothers. You see, I was not my mother's only child. I had a set of twin brothers three years older than I am; my mother not only had her first child at the age of fifteen but God gave her the gift of twins at that young age. At the time she was not able to raise them, so I didn't grow up with my brothers; instead their paternal grandmother took them and raised them just two blocks away from where we lived. It was very upsetting to me that my mother took in her cousin Rod and let him live with us after her aunt Amelia Simmons died. It was very weird and something I could not understand as a child. I was confused whenever I would see my brothers and talk to them but then they would go to another place which they called home. Why couldn't Rod go live somewhere else and let my brothers stay with us? I wondered how my mother was able to raise me and not all of us and why she took in her cousin and didn't go back for her sons. Why did we not live together? Rod was not my brother; he was just my mother's cousin. As a child it didn't matter to me that Rod didn't have his mother or father. All I knew was my mother was not his mother; she belonged to me, Craig, and Greg. I was always angry. I didn't like my cousin because I felt at times that he was flaunting the exact same thing in my brothers' faces, and many times I didn't like my mother and I would be rebellious because of the situation. I lived with this anger and never got over it until just a couple of years ago because I felt like my two brothers were visitors in our house when they came around. I had to repent, ask forgiveness, and let go of all the animosity I felt towards him. My cousin Rod, I know you have been in and out of the hospital, and I pray for your healing.

My mother was the best mother that she knew how to be to me, and she did whatever she could to give me everything she could. Eventually I understood on my own that my mother was too young when she had my brothers and by the time she was more mature and working the twins were attached to their grandmother. It took a lot of courage to let them continue to stay with their grandmother, but she was a good woman and raised them well.

My mom and I lived in an apartment in Washington Heights. We called the area the Dominican Republic because it had more Dominicans than any other race. It was weird.... You know how some people try to say all black people look alike? Well, I myself showed a little ignorance—I thought all Spanish-speaking people were the same and liked each other. But I learned very quickly that Puerto Ricans and Dominicans didn't get along.

I grew up on 160th Street in New York. There was a bar called Starlight on the corner where my mother, grandmother, and aunts all hung out. I was never allowed to go into the bar, so if I needed my mother for something I would always have to peep through the window and wait to get someone's attention and then Mom would come out. My godmother Tommy was the barmaid there. She reminded me of a big version of Flo from Mel's Diner on the '70s TV show *Alice*. Tommy had the white hair up in a beehive and was a very beautiful plus-size woman, with skin so light she could pass for Caucasian. She served drinks and made a ton of money, but she lived alone. On Sunday mornings, I would deliver my mom's homemade meals to Tommy and she would give me my allowance.

Starlight was the place to be in our neighborhood. All the adults would dress up just to go to that corner bar. There were fights there, but everyone knew each other so they would just take the beat-up person home when it was all over. There was also a drag queen named Phillip that used to hang out there. All the regulars knew about the cross dressing, but one day my mother's cousin Billy came to visit. My grandma, great-aunt Harriet, and my mother all watched Billy buying drinks for this drag queen. Well, everyone thought Billy knew because it was so obvious with the Adam's apple and all—I guess it was obvious to a person without alcohol in his system. Well, the night was going to be a long one, so with his high heels on Phillip decided to go home and change his clothes. You see, he went out the door as a woman; however, he came back in the door as a man. When cousin Billy realized the man and the "woman" were one and the same person and that he'd been spending his money on another man with a package between his legs, he lost it and beat that man's tail. Lucky for him back then they did not have the gay-bashing laws in place. That place was such a tight-knit hangout that it wasn't even pursued. He had to of course pay the bill and they all made friends before they parted ways. I guess the guy knew he was partly to blame for not letting Billy know up front and allowing him to make a choice.

My mom's two-bedroom apartment on 160th was the party house. Back in the '80s there would be a party every weekend— complete with drugs, cussing, and all kinds of people. My mom grew up around and made friends with all kinds: the gay men, the crackhead women, the alcoholics, the abused women. Drugs were just a way of life and so out in the open. I never saw them actually use drugs, but I did see the after-effects, and I knew it was cocaine coupled with the hangovers, and there were always empty Heineken bottles and cigarette butts lying around and drinking straws with the tips cut off. My mother's breath would reek of tomato juice from all the Bloody Marys she'd drunk the night before. These people would sometimes party all the way through the next day.

Looking back, I can say my mother was not the *Leave It to Beaver* mother, and I definitely didn't grow up in the best of environments. It may sound crazy, but she loved me and gave her very best to me. Because of that, I didn't realize the seriousness of the situations we encountered. Her boyfriend, Jack, was an alcoholic. It was so bad that even when he was not physically drinking he smelled strongly of alcohol. As a child I can remember people saying the alcohol smell was coming through his pores as he sweated. As soon as my mother hooked up with him she graduated from just alcohol to using and being around hard-core drugs.

One weekend in the summer, my mom, Jack, and my family had gone to New Jersey to visit Great Adventures theme park. When we came home late that evening we found Jack's kids, little Jack and his sister, sitting on the front steps of the building. They'd been left there early that day by their mother, Lonnie. That was a major surprise. She just dropped them off and never came back for them. They didn't have any clothes or anything, but she was making them move in with us into our two-bedroom apartment. Thank goodness that didn't last very long. When school started, their uncle came and took them to stay with him until Lonnie eventually went back to get them. I just found out from my mom that although Jack and Lonnie were separated for many years they were not divorced. God rest Jack's soul. He passed away in 2008 from a heart attack while at work.

I remember this white girl, Nancy, who lost her kids. They lived with their father, her ex-husband. Nancy had rotten teeth in her mouth but would always smile and loved to talk to you. At the time she was going out with this Spanish man who completely controlled her. He did allow her to visit our house though. On Nancy's paydays, he would meet her, collect most of her earnings, and just give her back some spending money. I don't know what ever happened to Nancy. I have seen so many of these people come and go and drop out of sight. I never understood how anyone could just be okay with not having their kids. When does enough become enough? Now I know that the ex-husband had to protect his kids because their mother was on drugs.

My mom had another friend, George, who was gay. George was always sharp, wearing a pair of white shoes, either patent leather or slip-ons like Tubbs wore on *Miami Vice*. He was flamboyant too, with his fast walk with a little twitch in his hips. George had a handsome old man named John. John played the role of the man while George wanted to sit home and be the woman out of the two; he was even on welfare for a while. He wore John out, always spending up his money and never paying the bills. John would have to take care of them. Those two were always breaking up, and George would come crying to my mom, later getting back with John. I only saw John once. He had long straight hair and was a nice-looking man. John didn't run the streets. I'm not sure if he even partied. I think back then in that society you didn't just pick up men in a bar. Of course that was not a rule George followed. This was at the time of the AIDS outbreak. Almost every month when George visited he would tell my mother about another friend of his that died with AIDS. I was young at the time, so I really didn't know how awful that was. But I remember that after George left, my mother would always throw out whatever glass he'd used that day. Maybe it was pure ignorance and not knowing. She didn't stop being his friend, but she also wanted to take precautions. It breaks my heart to say George died a few years ago. He was funny, always making jokes and looking not through his glasses but over them. I can still see him bending his head down to look at me over the rims of those glasses. He really is missed.

In the '70s and '80s all of the women in my family, an entire generation, were on welfare except my mother. I applaud each and every one of them for being good mothers. And don't think they were all unmarried; I watched two of my aunts who were married and still had to run the household on what little welfare income they got because their men were slouches. My aunts made me always want to strive to do better.

When I was young, I dreamed of going to college and then law school. I knew that somehow I would make my own way in life. I am the product of living with a single mother and am now a single mother myself, but I have always been determined to break this generational curse off of my family. I was determined not to be a damsel in distress. I was determined that, although I had four children, I would not be labeled the queen of welfare—you know the ones sitting at home having all those babies so the system can take care of them while they buy all the name-brand clothes that come into style and all the jewelry to go along with it (for themselves and not for the children, of course). I was determined to work as many jobs as necessary in order to become a strong woman and good mother.

Being a female in a man's world was a piece of cake to me because I could work twelve- or fourteen-hour days just like any man. I could run with the best of them, at times being better because of my "female advantage." You all know what I mean—we females have a way of getting what we want. I'm proud to say I didn't have to sleep with anyone's husband to succeed.

At the end of the day I am so glad my mother raised me as a single parent. I might not have been in the best of environments since my mother's house was the hangout spot, but what she never realized was that God had another plan for her life as well as for mine. He kept her and the people in her house from overdosing; he kept them out of jail. My mother was delivered by God. You see, the drugs were like a phase she was going through. She never went into any rehabilitation center, but one day God took the taste away from her, he blessed her and gave her a new start on life. Thank God she never touched drugs again. The urges were gone; you couldn't even get her to take a drink, let alone do drugs. Thank you, God, for delivering her. I did not have to grow up in a home with a verbally abusive parent—that would be my father, but let's save him for the next chapter.

Chapter 2

My Dad Always Dressed
Like a Pimp

My dad wasn't in my life much as I was growing up. I only remember him popping up for a few hours whenever he would come to New York for some other business. He would always give me twenty or fifty dollars when he left, but being young, I didn't know that didn't mean much or take care of much of anything. He certainly contributed to my young life being filled with confusion and left me nearly emotionless. At one point in my adult life I did not know how to reciprocate love.

I used to ride the Trailways bus to visit my dad in Maryland. My mom always put me on the bus and I had to sit in the seat next to the bus driver. Both my dad and stepmother drove, but neither of them would ever come pick me up.

I would get jealous every time I visited because I would see the house they all lived in and would just be thinking that my mom and I didn't have all this. They were in a different home nearly every year I visited, and that made me so angry. I thought my half brother and stepsister must have it made to be able to move to a different house every year. But perception is not the truth, and matters are not always what they seem. It turned out that my dad didn't have very good financial status and they were forced to move a lot because they could not afford the houses they lived in.

I was really lucky I did not grow up with them, and I thank God that my mom was able to raise me. My dad and stepmom had a very dysfunctional household. I remember one Thanksgiving when I was about thirteen or fourteen, I visited them and we all sat at the dinner table with no one talking to each other. All you could hear was forks hitting the plates. It was terrible. At my mother's house the whole family would be talking and watching football or playing cards until the food was ready. Trust me, it was never quiet. We even did our own version of open mic, singing songs on the radio, and we kids did our Jackson 5 act and danced and entertained until it was time to eat. It was truly a lively, loving atmosphere. But this year at my father's house all you could hear was the forks and knives hitting the plates. Then my dad went to cut the ham and somehow it fell on the floor. Immediately I started laughing. To me that was hilarious, but everybody else just sat there. They all talked and laughed about it as soon as my dad left the room though, which shows you how much dominance he actually had in his own house.

Another time I remember my dad with his mean self trying to start a fire in the cast iron oven they had in their house. He kept poking at the fire, and it eventually jumped out and nearly caught him on fire. He was lucky God spared him, but his eyebrows and the front of his hair was burned off.

My father always put his wife down and was always talking about her, being very verbally abusive to her. I grew up feeling sorry for her. I remember he would always say things like "you stink." Even though she smoked cigarettes, there was always something about the way he said it to her. Then one day when I was grown I finally told my half brother I had no respect for his mother, that she was spineless and all I could remember were the abusive things my dad would always say to her. She would always take his side against us kids even if she knew he was wrong. I never saw her stand up to my father.

One summer my dad thought everyone had gone down to North Carolina for my stepmother's family reunion. Actually everyone went except my brother, but my dad didn't know that. My brother later told me he came home from school that day and found another woman in his mother's bed. My dad told him, "Oh, that's your mother. She doesn't feel well, so go ahead and leave her alone." He said this without hesitation. What he didn't count on was my brother actually talking to his mother on the phone. Of course she was in North Carolina. I would have thought that was the straw to break the camel's back, but still she stayed with him. I thought she was the most forgiving of women. What I didn't realize then was that she was a very weak woman and my dad most likely crushed her self-esteem. As I became older I had to pray for my stepmother and pray for God to forgive me because of the way I felt about her. She tried to make my stepsister out to be my father's child, but she wasn't. I listened to my stepsister call my father "Dad," and I would say, "That's not your father. Why do you do that?" I could never bring myself to call him dad; I guess it was because I never felt very close to him or even relaxed around him. I would call him Mr. Craft or not make any reference to him by name, just jump right into the conversation as soon as I had his attention.

I always thought my dad didn't like my stepsister. He would talk to her mean and treat her bad. At times I couldn't understand why her mother would allow it. Why didn't she leave my dad? If you don't like my children or you treat them bad, I don't care who you are or what you have, you are out of here. I used to be so angry that my stepmother would not speak up for her daughter, and I said I would never let a man do that, I didn't care if it was their natural father or not. I truly feel my dad was ashamed of my stepsister and never wanted to take her anywhere because she was always husky and my stepmother didn't know how to do hair. The girl kept a nappy head and would have two ponytails with a crooked part, one side higher than the other. My mom didn't know how to do hair either, but that's what Ms. May the hairdresser was for. I would go to her to get my hair pressed with the hot comb and curled. I remember I always had to make sure it didn't get wet or it would become nappy again. At times I felt really bad because my dad was big on appearances. Shoot, his hair was long and he used to perm it so he looked like Reverend Al Sharpton. His nails were long but he kept them clean. Back then my dad looked like what we now call a PIMP. I could tell he disliked it when he had to take my stepsister out; it was almost like she was the ugly stepsister. I'm not saying she was ugly though, because to me she wasn't. I thought she was a beautiful young lady. It made me so angry when my dad would tear her down—he was a real verbal abuser—and her mother just let him say whatever he wanted.

My stepsister would be happy playing and laughing, but one time when my dad came in the house my stepsister wet herself. My aunt said she told my grandma she wondered if my dad was beating her. Something must have happened to make the girl so scared she would literally wet herself when she saw him. Another time she even ran under her mother's skirt she was so scared to look at my dad. I know she got in trouble for everything when we were little.

I thought these people had so much, when in reality they had nothing but craziness, a very unstable house—and what I've told you so far isn't even the half of it. My aunt Glowie told me that when my dad lived in the Bronx, she would babysit while his wife worked. Keep in mind I have never been to a wedding, my aunt said she has never been to a wedding, nor have any of my dad's sisters and brothers. However, one year the status changed from Sharon the girlfriend to now they were married.

I realize now that my stepmother was in an abusive relationship. My dad used to hit her. I have some memories of this, and my aunt Glowie confirms it. My stepmother thought my grandmother Louise and aunt Glowie didn't notice the black eyes she would always try to cover up, but Aunt Glowie told me she most certainly did notice. I never saw my dad and her physically fight; however, I'm certain he used to let my stepsister and my brother see the fights happen since they lived in the same house. My brother had so much anger and hate built up in him, as soon as he was old enough he went head-on at my father. It was so bad that my brother went into the military straight out of high school just to leave home. Knowing my stepmother was in an abusive relationship helped me understand why she did what she did back then; however, I didn't understand why she never got fed up.

I would like to close for now and continue on to the next chapter, but not before I mention my godfather, Ike. He was a very flamboyant openly gay man, with plenty of money; however, he took great interest in my father. He would buy my dad anything, and indeed my dad asked for the most expensive gifts. He received cars, clothes—my dad kept money because of Ike. That was a relationship I could never understand; I didn't understand how it evolved. Ike was no relation to our family. He and my dad did their hair alike, but right before Ike passed away my dad wasn't speaking to him. During the last conversation I had with Ike, the only thing he told me was my dad had stolen money from him and he didn't have to do it because he would have given my father anything he asked for.

Chapter 3

Sister Just Two Blocks Over

⁓

My uncle BooBoo (sadly and funny to say, I don't even know what his actual name was—he died with me calling him and only knowing him as Uncle BooBoo) was my father's other brother. There were a total of six kids in that family—Grandma Louise was two kids busier than I was.

Uncle BooBoo would always stop by and say hello to me, even though he and my dad hated each other. BooBoo would always tell me, "Your dad ain't s***. My brother Sylvester ain't s***." He made it clear to me that he hated my dad but he loved me because I was his niece. He was an alcoholic but also the nicest, kindest man you could ever meet; he was not a nasty drunk (the kind who want to fight when they drink) but a kind one. You knew he drank because you could actually smell the liquor every time he would hug you or come very close to you; he drank so much it came out through his pores. He was also very funny and always made me laugh. Uncle BooBoo wasn't the type that would give me money or candy, but every time I saw him I knew I would get a laugh.

One day my uncle told me that I had a sister that lived on 158th. Mind you, I grew up on 160th, so that was literally just two streets over. He was drinking at the time, but I knew he would be truthful. Later I asked my dad about it, saying, "Dad, Uncle BooBoo told me I had a sister that lives two blocks over." His response was "That's a lie. BooBoo is an alcoholic, a drunk bum that doesn't know what he is talking about." So I said okay because I was thinking that maybe BooBoo was mixed up and was actually talking about my stepsister. Then Uncle BooBoo told me once again, "You got a sister that lives on 158th Street." I just told him, "Okay, Uncle BooBoo, whatever you say." I could tell because he kept saying it over and over to me that it was not about my stepsister. I asked my dad again, and he said BooBoo was a lying drunk that didn't know what he was talking about.

Uncle BooBoo died—I believe it was of cirrhosis of the liver—but about ten years later I was visiting my father and they told me that my sister had come to visit. I just looked at them like they had two heads. Who were they talking about? Well, turned out it was the same girl that lived just two blocks over from me. Uncle BooBoo was right. The one problem I had was with my father; he lied to me and took away any opportunity I may have had to meet my own sister. I was very angry. I walked past that street every day to get to my school, so I'm sure I may have seen this girl many times. Sad to say I do not know what she looks like to this day. I got so angry with the way my dad had treated my uncle, calling him a liar and a drunk and making me distrust BooBoo. All that time I believed my father, but it turned out he was the liar. He denied my ever having a sister, and at the point that he wanted to now admit it I didn't care to meet her. Again I looked at my stepmother and told my brother, "Your mother … how does she just let him bring a kid around and say, 'This is my teenage daughter; she's spending time with us'?" Wow.

I was told back then that my dad used to hang out in the motorcycle club with Aunt Bernadette's husband and he met this woman and slept with her. Guys, that's not true. They try to make it sound like a one-night stand and it was not. My aunt Glowie used to babysit my "secret sister." Aunt Glowie would stay overnight in their apartment whenever my dad took this girl's mother out. This child's mother was my dad's mistress, and he took care of her for a very long time. It wasn't until she started stepping out on him that he ended it. I was hurt because I didn't see my father that often, but now I knew he was coming to New York and did not bother to see me all the time. He was seeing my sister I never met because he was sleeping with her mother. He would bring all the women he slept with and messed around with to Grandma Louise's house—I mean quite a few—while his wife Sharon was downtown. Guess what? I don't feel the least bit sorry for Sharon. Ironically, my mom caught my father cheating on her with Sharon at Grandma Louise's house. So now my dad has done the same thing to her and cheated with other women, bringing them back to the very same place it started with her. So what goes around comes around.

Sometime in the mid-1990s, my dad brought the girl around, according to my stepmother. The girl was very ghetto acting and disrespectful. I could not understand why she was there. They spoke so badly about her afterwards. I never accepted this newfound relationship, at least not the way my stepmother and the others did. I was so angry and hurt; my dad had betrayed me. I have to say it again so you can understand how I felt for years throughout my childhood: My father denied having other children, particularly another daughter. Now since you are ready to talk about it, now that you are ready to have her come around because you want to admit it all of a sudden then I'm supposed to just accept it like it's okay. Well it's not, and I really couldn't understand what in the heck Sharon was thinking. It also turned out that my sister who lived two streets over was in a relationship with my little elementary school boyfriend that I had gone out with for over a year. I will give him the benefit of the doubt that he didn't know we were sisters; heck, I didn't even know. Best of all, we were just graduating elementary school entering into junior high school and never experienced sex.

Just recently I learned something else while speaking with my aunt Glowie. Grandma Louise had a party one night. Around 2 a.m., Glowie was out on the building steps with a friend and told BooBoo good night as he was leaving to go home. Glowie went inside the apartment to use the bathroom, and suddenly her friend ran in to tell everyone her brothers were fighting. Glowie was the first back out the door, followed by Grandma Louise and everyone else. Booboo was bleeding from a cut over his eye. My father had hit him with a beer bottle. Thank goodness the bottle didn't break or it would have been much worse. Glowie asked them why they were fighting, but neither one of them would say. Grandma jumped in and said to my father, "Don't you ever come to my house and put your hands on my son again." Glowie told Uncle BooBoo he had to go to the hospital. He kept insisting he was okay, but she finally made him go. It turned out he had to get about six stitches over his eye.

Now after Aunt Glowie and I spoke we both put two and two together. We think my dad attacked my uncle because he told me about my sister. And that wasn't the only time my father's other kids came up in an argument.

In 1999 when I first separated from my ex-husband, I was staying with my dad for a while and one day I sat there and watched him and my half brother nearly get into a fistfight. My dad told him to get out of his house, saying he had another son anyway. He said his son was in the military and he didn't need my half brother. I just looked at my father, but what made me angry was once again my stepmother didn't say anything to my dad; she didn't take up for her own son, let alone herself, when he said he had more children. My kids were there too, and they were so nervous since they were not used to all of the yelling and fighting that was going on. So as it turned out, I may have quite a few siblings out there from Mr. Craft.

Chapter 4

My School Days

I went to elementary school at PS 28, the Wright Brothers School, on 155th Street and Amsterdam Avenue. Those were the wonder years and the best years I spent at a school. I was on the track team and the drama team, and just recently through the technology of Facebook I was able to reunite with some old friends like the sisters Tonia and Tamela Davis of 159th Street and Jeff Terry with the green eyes of 158th Street and St. Nicholas Avenue. We have been reminiscing on all of the good times there and locating other students. I found out recently I was a popular young lady back then. It was such a family-knit environment I didn't realize all the young men that admired me until now.

I was recently blessed with the opportunity to reconnect with at least one of the teachers, my drama teacher, Ms. Joyce Greenleaf, and tell her thank you. Those elementary school years were the building blocks of my life's foundation, and I thanked Ms. Greenleaf for sowing her time and talent which have played a part in helping me become the woman I am today. The teachers in those days really cared about us. We were scared to get out of line because they had no problem with scolding us and then telling our parents so we would get scolded again. Every parent knew every teacher, and we kids knew better than to get out of line. The sad thing is you don't have too many teachers that can be that way today because they would lose their job, or even worse, with so much violence in the school system now they may risk getting attacked.

I went to junior high school at Roberto Clemente IS 195 on 133rd Street and Broadway. One time I got into trouble because my friend brought her uncle's BB gun to school and one of our other friends thought we were going to shoot her with it. Mom ended up having to come to the school, which turned out not to be so good for me.

I remember the highlight of everyone's summers would be the block parties held on 159th Street. Busy Bee was the host for quite a few years and each year was better than the last. In the daytime there would be carnival games and kids playing in the water thanks to the fire department going out to put a sprinkler cap on the fire hydrant. You would hear Spanish music playing and people would be eating, talking, and dancing. When the sun went down it was time to party. We would put on the best outfits—it was a fashion show, hair was done up, and we would go out there and mingle and party. People would come from all over—Uptown, Downtown, Harlem, the Bronx, Yonkers—everyone would be in the streets listening to music until the block party was over. So many people would go through and support the community block party. DJ Kid Capri, Doug E. Fresh, Big Daddy Kane, Biz Markie, Fat Joe, Magic Johnson, and the list goes on. Each year you could count on having a good time.

During those same years, the guys used to play dice across the street from the building I lived in. They called the game C-Lo. Of course it was illegal, so whenever they would see the police coming they would stop and look around like they weren't doing anything. This one day they were so busy listening to Notorious B.I.G., Doug E. Fresh, and RUN DMC music being played on the radio and battling each other (rapping along) the police caught them, called me over, and told them to give me all the money they had. It was hilarious. My uncle Justin and his friends were pleading with me and trying to make me give them back the money when the police left.

I remember the days we would just hang out on the building's front stoop and listen to DJ Red Alert 98.7 Kiss FM and Wendy Williams, also on 98.7 Kiss FM. There was this one time my entire family was hanging out on the stoop outside. I was about twenty-one and pregnant with Brittney, my second child. I got off the stoop to go inside the house to get some water and to use the bathroom. Well, as I opened the door to my mom's first-floor apartment there was a boy running down the hall and he ran straight inside. I'm standing there like "What the H-E-double-hockey-sticks is he doing?" Moments later there was banging on the door. I stepped into the bathroom, and then the front door was kicked in. I was so blessed that God covered me because it was the police chasing this boy with guns drawn. He'd just run into the first opening he saw, my mother's apartment. Thank God the police didn't shoot, but I will tell you he got one big butt-whooping for making them chase him and making them have to repair the door once they found out he didn't live there or know us.

On another occasion we were down in my grandmother Caroline's building when we suddenly heard this great big boom. Turned out there was a group of drug dealers that lived in the apartment above and one of them let their gun go off. My uncle Anthony was lying in bed at the time, and the shot just missed his head; the bullet hole was inches away in the ceiling. We called the police, but those guys ran out of there so fast and they had a steel door, so we thought it was impossible for the police to get in. They never did catch them and the guys never came back again, but this was in the days of the infamous Dirty 30, when a precinct was temporarily shut down and the officers there were replaced with officers from different parts of the state. Worst of all, several officers were arrested for being corrupt (dirty). The police from the Thirty-fourth Precinct came back to the apartment later that day and were trying to get into it. We thought at the time they were determined to get the guys, but it turned out they were just trying to rob them and get the drugs.

As kids, we liked to play in cars. My mother's friend Jerry always let me play in his car and sit on his motorcycle up until the time when I was about ten and one day my cousin and I were sitting in the car and I was playing with the steering wheel and pretending to drive—"Vroom vroom!" Well, me and my smart self decided to pull the gear shift down. Suddenly everyone was yelling and running to the car, and there I was rolling down the street scared as I don't know what. Jerry was hanging inside the car trying to get to the emergency brake. Needless to say I never got back into his car to play ever again, and thank God by his grace there wasn't anyone hurt.

It was about three years later that I got my start in sales. My mother's boyfriend back then, Jack, used to work for Fieldcrest, which was huge in the bathroom items. Jack used to bring home bath towels, wash cloths, and hand towels, and would let me sell them and keep half the money. Jack was using me. I would go door to door selling these items to all our Hispanic neighbors, who loved to buy from little thirteen-year-old me. I would sell out every time.

Although this was all for Jack's gain, he actually did help me because I learned so much back then that I can still apply in my current sales job. He was just lucky I wasn't business savvy, or it would not have been 50/50 but more like 60/40—Hey, I was doing all the work!

The one problem I encountered was with the man that lived on the third floor. He would always buy towels from me, and it had gotten to the point that he would buy everything I had. One day I saw him in passing in the hallway and he gave me some money, around sixty dollars. I thought he wanted to prepay for the next order that was coming in, but he stopped taking the towels. I went to drop the order off at the apartment where he lived with his wife and kids (of course I never went inside; I would always stand in the hallway), but when I knocked on the door he told me to keep the towels. And then he reached in his pocket and gave me one hundred dollars. What I didn't realize was that he was giving me money to buy things I wanted. I was taking it—no harm, no foul—and God was covering me again from what could have turned into a really bad situation. This man was gaining my trust, and God blocked whatever ill intentions he was planning with me as I was definitely a minor. Needless to say, I became uncomfortable and stopped selling him the towels.

I also learned how to gamble back then. On the weekends all of my family—aunts, uncles, brothers, cousins—and family friends would come over to Grandma Caroline's house. I particularly remember a few of the men folk; there were these two brothers, Eric and Herbie, and then there was Mike (Strong) and Dennis (Denny Moe). We would play draw poker, and at times the pots got to be pretty big. It was fun, but playing with your family is the worst. When you beat them and win the money, they want to keep borrowing from you to continue playing and try to win back the same money you just won. My brother Bubba was the best at that. We would tell him to go home; he would lose money and then owe more from borrowing. He was always good though because the next game he had to pay off what he owed before he could play with us again.

Bubba was so funny. He is a small man who loved plus-size women and always wanted to play matchmaker with the rest of the guys but, although nothing is wrong with the larger women, he was the only one that was into that type. The guys would tell him, "Heck no, I'm not going out with you." He would talk about these women like they were gifts to men. Bubba was exactly like the guy in the movie *Shallow Hal*; what he saw and what everyone else saw were two completely different things. Bubba and his twin brother would cut up and cuss each other out once they started going back and forth about women.

Then there was my uncle. Believe me when I tell you he was such a smooth talker. He would let me hang out with him and his friends in the music industry because he wanted to use the jewelry my kids' dad bought me. When I was still in high school I had the big triangle earrings and the big rope chains like Run-DMC (that was when I believed my children's father when he told me his family owned a jewelry store), so whenever Doug E. Fresh had a video shoot my uncle would take me along just so he could use my jewelry. I even traveled and went to a couple of concerts in different states. Once Doug E. Fresh was on the stage performing in Philadelphia when suddenly all the lights and power was cut. He'd been doing good. In my opinion he was sounding better than Wil Smith, who was also one of the performers on the show, and I always thought Wil played a role in having those lights turned off to make the show end early, especially since he ran Philly at the time. I have also gone to shows and been backstage with the likes of LL Cool J, Teddy Riley, and Tony Tone Toni. I would always go anticipating running into the one rapper I grew up having a very big crush on. That man was one of the smoothest rappers out, NAS. Although he always looked like he was feeling really good (if you know what I mean), I thought he was so handsome and I had the biggest crush on him. Unfortunately, every time he was in the company of my uncle I was always in the middle of something that I couldn't drop. Since my uncle told the kids about my big crush, until this day if my kids see him on the television they call me to come watch. It was amazing but sad to see the groupies line up at the hotels afterwards, ready to do anything just to get in. My uncle had *so* many women; he better realize how God covered him, because he is still here. I know for a fact he didn't use protection, because there are at least twenty kids out here with mothers claiming that he is the father. If I remember correctly, he claims about four kids with four different baby mamas. I used to tease my uncle because he had so many girls but they were not all the best-looking women. Some of them looked like men, but he would mesmerize them and they would give him everything and pay for whatever he wanted. My family couldn't even talk these women out of it.

I love my uncle. He hasn't changed, maybe slowed down with the women, but he's still always at every party and concert you could imagine. He's got to be at least fifty, yet not long ago my oldest daughter said, "Ma, I saw Uncle Justin talking to a girl in her twenties." LOL—He lies so much about his age, I really don't think even he knows his own age. He's been thirty years old for the last twenty years. The best thing about Uncle Justin is that nothing bothers him. You can cuss him out, say no to him for something, and he will turn right back around and ask for it again. He knows everyone. In fact, his friends once laughed because he went backstage and knew the guys at a heavy metal rock concert. They bet him he couldn't get in—and of course they lost. Uncle Justin always has someone to chauffeur him around and has never in his life had a driver's license. My uncle Tony teases him that my kids, his two great-nieces Tiff and Britt, have had driver's licenses since they were sixteen years old and he still doesn't have a license. Guess what? He doesn't care; he just asks Tiff and Britt to drive him around too!

Chapter 5

House Party

━◠

This chapter is dedicated to the memories of Juggler, Caroline, Donnell, Falo, Dot, Joaquin, Cookie, and Nathan (Pops).

I grew up with my grandmother always hosting different events from Thanksgiving dinner to our infamous Fourth of July picnic on the Hudson (Riverside Drive). Fourth of July was always a long day's work. You see, since you could see the fireworks being shot from the water we always had to send someone to wait in line for the park to open and get us a great spot. There would be a lot of people; it would always be just as packed as if you were on the beach in ninety-five-degree weather. Somehow our spot would always be the place everyone would look for. This was because they all knew once they found the Singletons they could find the fixings of great food. See, our cookouts were not just hot dogs and hamburgers. Oh no—it was like Thanksgiving in July. We would have corn on the cob, potato salad, green beans, steak, ribs, chicken, and Nathan's Famous Hot Dogs from Coney Island. Our guests included Puerto Ricans and Dominicans, black people and white people—our picnics were always interracial.

Speaking of Spanish people, one year my grandpa and Falo, the son of the Spanish family that lived in the building next to my grandparents', were supposed to go find a nice spot by the water and then stay there until the rest of the group arrived. The good news was they found a nice location and set up our picnic table. The bad news was when they finished setting up the table Pops went to pull the truck off of the grass and ran over the picnic table. Yes, he backed right into it. By the time we got to the park Pops and Falo had done a repair job, tying the table back together with some rope. When my grandma asked what happened to the table the two of them said they didn't know.

The picnics were always a blast. We would play spades and all the kids would go to the park and play basketball or tag until the food was ready. Sometimes we'd just go stand near the water (Hudson River) and throw rocks in it, watch all the people out on the water in the boats and on jet skis, then at night we would watch as they would shoot off the fireworks, and the sky would light up so beautifully.

Getting back to reality, I grew up in a neighborhood infested with drug dealers and illegal immigrants. Almost every evening we heard gunshots being fired or saw someone getting arrested. It was a very noisy place. All of us kids would always be taken care of and watched out for. Our family would always make sure the kids were safe; everyone looked out for each other. Even the drug dealers would try to keep us kids out of harm's way. I did, however, get the chance to see one live gunfight when I was about eleven or twelve years old.

There were these two brothers from Cuba, one named Cookie and the other named Joaquin. Cookie was this skinny, dark-skinned Cuban, and Joaquin was the older brother who walked with a limp and was always drinking. My family would speak with them outside and we came to know them. They told us how they came to America in the 1980s. They were in a Cuban jail and were put on a boat with just the clothes on their backs. After doing my research on the exile back then, I remember watching on the news about what had been done. Castro loaded boats with prison inmates and psychiatric patients. Cookie and Joaquin were part of a boatload of more than 120,000 Cubans. Since they'd been in jail in Cuba and by all means were no strangers to trouble, they weren't afraid of it when it came.

We were all sitting on the front steps of the building when suddenly Cookie ran by and told us, "Get in the house. There's going to be trouble." Before we could get all the way into the building Cookie started shooting at this man. No one knew who it was, but in the middle of the two of them shooting at one another and no one getting hit fortunately Cookie's gun jammed. When Joaquin saw that Cookie had gun problems, he then jumped in and started shooting his gun. I remember the gun because it looked like something Clint Eastwood would use—it was big. The police came after it was all over. That was the usual back then; they never arrested anyone. Of course out of all the people there, no one would speak as a witness. That's what they did in those days, protect each other.

It was the same way one other night when a poker game got out of hand and turned bloody. Ms. Dee was the neighbor that lived one floor below my grandmother. She was in a tough spot and didn't have money to pay her rent. I was six years old at the time my grandmother put together a poker party in which a percentage of every hand would go into a different pot for what they called the house. This was to raise money to help Ms. Dee with her rent. All of the kids were up in my grandma's house again just one floor up.

There was this guy named Lucky who had lost all of his money and wanted them to give it back to him. Well, of course that was not going to happen. At the poker game my grandma sold dinners and they had plenty of alcohol. Apparently his drinking brought out the worst in him. Lucky got mad and went on a rampage, attacking everyone with a big knife as sharp and large as a machete. My dad had on a wide-brim hat just like Super Fly (actor Ron O' Neal) wore in the movies. This night that outfit might very well have saved his life. Lucky swung the knife at my father and it cut right through the brim of his hat, taking it off. He stabbed my great-aunt Harriet in the head (Harriet at the time was seeing Lucky's son). When he swung at Grandma she went to put her arms up to cover her face and head and the knife nearly cut off her hand. He cut Juggler too. My great-uncle Banov was in the bathroom. Lucky took his bloodbath down the hall, kicked in the bathroom door, and stabbed Uncle Banov repeatedly. Juggler, God rest his soul, had a gun but couldn't get a clear shot at Lucky. My mother and Aunt Ann both said there was blood spurting from Banov's wounds. Lucky ran out of the house, and with all the confusion of everyone trying to get medical attention they didn't follow behind him. Well, he didn't go home or run into hiding; instead, covered in blood, he went to the neighborhood bar and sat down to drink. Everyone was trying to help him because they thought the blood was his and that he may have been attacked.

Another very close friend of the family heard what happened. Word got out quickly, and Donnell arrived before the police could get to the Starlight bar to get Lucky. Donnell went in with his .22-caliber gun, went right up to Lucky, and opened fire. He emptied the gun on him, the final shot going through Lucky's cheek. Donnell ran out of the bar before the police came, but Lucky stayed there drinking. Every time he would take a drink he would spit up blood. Lucky wouldn't tell the police what happened to him, and neither would anyone else. Donnell went down south and Lucky never came around again. No one was arrested and no charges were pressed. You see, justice was different back in 1976. None of the people in the house wanted Lucky to go to jail; they were just looking for him to take matters into their own hands. All of the kids were crying when we saw the blood. I remember all of us but especially my uncle saying he couldn't wait until he grew up so he could kill Lucky for cutting Grandma Caroline. Lucky died a few years ago from cancer.

Chapter 6

Aunt Ann: My Babysitter and Encourager

My favorite aunt, Ann, was always beautiful, athletic, strong willed, and fashionable. Aunt Ann used to babysit me while my mother worked. I would be with her all day every day until she became an army wife and started to travel often. Even then she was my babysitter.

When I was around nine years old my mother let me fly out to Savannah, Georgia, to spend the summer with my aunt. This was the first time I flew on an airplane. I remember having a lot of fun that summer. It was also my very first trip to Florida's Walt Disney World. We drove down to visit Mickey Mouse at his home. I was so excited to meet Mickey, Minnie, and Goofy. It was a great trip and everyone had fun.

I never told Aunt Ann what I'm about to say until just recently. I wanted to let her know about this incident from my own lips instead of reading it in the book. She lived in a townhouse with a first-floor patio door that opened up to an in-ground swimming pool. There was a huge sign warning that you would not be allowed in the pool area if a lifeguard was not on site. One day during my visit, my aunt thought I was outside playing with the other kids in the area, but I was actually alone. I decided to do what any typical child would do—I went into the pool. Everything was fine at first. I stayed around the edges with my feet hanging in the pool. Then I went and sat on the stairs in the kiddie pool, and when I realized I could walk around the three-foot-deep part of the pool and the water only came up to my chest I was comfortable enough to do that. Then I decided I wanted to teach myself how to swim.

I started by trying to float and stay on top of the water. When that wasn't working, I decided to hold my breath while squatting in the water and just circling my arms. I did this for a while and was really getting the hang of it. As I was circling under water I lost sense of my location in the pool. I went to stand up, but when I did I couldn't get out of the water. This time it was over my head. I could look up and see the daylight, but I could not reach the surface. I didn't know at the time I was in the middle of drowning. I panicked and just kept flapping my arms and jumping up trying to rocket myself upwards from the bottom of the pool. That panicking motion is what saved me. I managed to float back over to the kiddie pool. I got out of the pool, went inside the house, and changed my clothes. I was scared to say something back then because I knew I would get into trouble; I was not supposed to be out there at all. The rest of the trip I was really quiet and stuck close to my aunt. I never even mentioned it to my mother until now because it's not like my aunt was not watching me; I was being sneaky and it nearly cost me my life.

I also recently spoke to Aunt Ann about another incident from years ago, and she could not believe that I remembered it. My aunt never drove, and since she lived in military housing she didn't stay that far from the commissary. Of course this was the countryside and we had to walk along a path through the woods to get there. One day we walked to the commissary to shop around. I remember my aunt would always buy the Mello Yello sodas. I used to love these lemon-lime sodas; they tasted great. Well, this day a strange man kept following us around the store trying to hit on my aunt. She clearly was not interested and told him so as nicely as she could. He didn't have on an army uniform, but I assumed he had to be affiliated with the military in order to be on the base. Well, after we shopped and left the base we were walking back through the trail and we noticed this man was following us. Even though I was young, I could sense that my aunt was scared. We walked as fast as we could to make it to the house. All I could think was that we could get inside and lock the doors. My aunt's husband was out in the field, so he couldn't help us if the man came inside. My aunt was nervous; she didn't let me see it, but still I sensed it. Thank God we made it to the house. When we got inside Aunt Ann didn't even take the groceries to the kitchen; she just dropped them by the front door and went in her bedroom. I started to follow her because I was scared, but she told me to stay there with the baby, my cousin Sheka. So I went back into the living room and sat in front of the television with Sheka. My aunt came down and unlocked the door. I didn't know what she was doing by going back out there. The man was standing on the other side of the street. Aunt Ann marched right up and stood face-to-face with him. Pretty soon he left and never came back around. When she came back in I understood what had happened. You see, her husband left a gun in the house in case of an emergency when he was in the field. Aunt Ann just let that man see the gun and told him she would not hesitate to use it if he stepped one foot near the house. I don't think she realized how dangerous that was, especially since she had all the adrenaline running. She didn't think I remembered that day until I just told her.

Regardless of how our family argued with one another, Aunt Ann always made sure family came first. My mother was the enforcer at that time; she would do all the fighting. She once fought a man for my uncle, and she didn't hesitate to fight or cut with a knife anyone that would mess with our family. My aunt Ann was the peacemaker. When my cousins would get arrested, she would rally everyone so that all the family would go down together and show the judge they had a supportive family. When my cousins were out there on drugs, we would wander the streets to look for them and try to bring them home. Aunt Ann spent the last days with my uncle Butch when he was dying. She would also go to all the graduations and awards ceremonies.

I remember when we found this one cousin that was really strung out on drugs, my aunt went over two hours away to take her to the drug rehab center in upstate New York. A couple of days later we were walking on Broadway and saw my cousin who was supposed to be in rehab. It turned out that she signed herself out of the rehabilitation center and hitchhiked back to the city.

When my aunt moved back to New York for good I was so happy she was home. She's such an important part of our family. Aunt Ann is one of the strong women who've kept this family going over the years. Strong women have played such a critical role in our family and set such an example for me. Where else would I have gotten the idea that I could be something other than a woman on welfare, that I could step out of that life where I'd been surrounded by drugs and violence? It was largely because of women like Aunt Ann that I saw a hopeful future for myself. I could picture myself as an attorney, with an education, living a successful life.

Well, things wouldn't turn out quite that way, and it would be a while before I truly got away from the drugs and violence, as you're about to see.

In closing, I must add my aunt Ann was also the family dentist. She would pull out every loose tooth any of us had. Her MO was to tell you to come and let her feel it and while she was talking to you she would mess with the tooth until she could get a grip on it and snatch it right out of your mouth. Being young, we didn't learn or know any better and would keep getting caught by her asking to just feel it. We all finally wised up, and it was so funny that later in life I watched Aunt Ann do the same thing to my children and all her great-nieces and -nephews.

Chapter 7

In Loving Memory of My Grandfather
Joe Nathan Singleton ("Chooch")
January 6, 1930 – October 19, 1987

⁓

When I was older and became successful in the car business to the point where I was making thousands of dollars each month, I thought it was my duty to help everyone that needed help. Where did I get this idea, and why didn't I know how to manage my own money? Well, I was never taught finances when I was younger. I was never taught about investments, savings, or credit. When I was growing up, our idea of credit was the neighborhood convenience store where we could go to Mr. Juan and run up a tab to get anything we needed, then once a month when the checks came in we squared the bill away. My grandparents' furniture was from the man that I saw come around once a month to collect the monthly payment due. They didn't sign any contracts; it was all done by a handshake.

· Although we didn't have much when I was younger, we had each other. My grandparents had a two-bedroom apartment where ten of us lived until I was about eight years old. This house was my version of the movie *Big Momma's House*. Eventually my father's uncle let my mom move into his apartment building on 160th, where she still lives to this day.

At my grandparents' house, there were certain people we only saw at holiday times, and no matter who they were my grandmother fed everyone; no one went away hungry. As kids we had no idea what my grandmother was doing. We used to get mad that the only time we saw most of these people was when they wanted to come eat. My grandmother was giving to all the strangers and friends, but she was a selfish woman towards my granddad. I remember they always slept in different beds; even though he was a very hardworking man and she was a housewife, she had the full-size bed and he slept on the bottom of one of the bunk beds.

I loved my grandfather, Pops, so much and I miss him. He was really the only male figure in my life. Pops was an alcoholic. In those days it was common that everyone hung out at the local bar, the one where my godmother was the barmaid. My granddad didn't do the bar scene, but I remember his drink was Seagram's gin and he smoked Camel cigarettes, the ones without the filter. Back then we were some bad little kids; we would find the bottles hidden (he never left them out in the open for us kids to see, but we would look for those bottles of gin) everywhere in the house, and each time we found it he would have to get a different hiding place. We used to pour out the liquor and fill the bottle up with water because we didn't like to see him drinking. I remember him yelling; his favorite words were "DAMN YA." And he would always bang on a table when he said it. Once we heard those words, we knew he'd found his liquor bottle filled with water. We found bottles in the cake pan, under the stove, in the flour pots; he used to try to put it in the cabinet and we had to be nosey and climb up on the shelf to find it. Although Pops ("Chooch" to all that knew him) was an alcoholic, he used to hug us, talk to us, tell us he loved us, but the one thing he could never do right was pronounce any of our names. If your name was Tiffanie he would call you Stephanie. My nickname was Tinge but he called me Timmy. My cousin Dysheka, he called her Deshiekie, and my cousin Jasmine, instead of Jas he called her Jazz up. And forget about Shanise; to him it was Sharese. Pops was very loving but always showed us tough love. If you were a boy and cried, he would say, "Shut up, you little punk, acting like a sissy." If we were complaining, he would ask us girls do we want cookies with our wine. He did it always with the best of intentions.

Whenever Pops would try to send us on an errand for him, he would say, "Go to the store and get me three Choco Bliss [his favorite]." Of course he would always follow up by saying, "You better not cross the street. You better get somebody to cross you, ya hear me now? I will tear ya jitty up if you don't do what I say!" ("Tear ya jitty up" meant we were going to get a beating.) The memory now just makes me smile. Why would you send us alone to a store that is on the opposite side of the street and tell us not to cross the street alone? Thinking back, we must have looked very foolish standing on the street corner watching the light turn green, yellow, and red over and over again and not walking across on the red, just waiting impatiently until someone that we knew came by so we could ask them to help us across the street.

My mother told me I was the only grandchild that sucked a pacifier and Pops did not like seeing it in my mouth. He would always throw it out of the window, and I would cry all night until my mother went and picked up a new one. They would be so mad at Pops because no one in the house could sleep.

I remember Pops would always come home and he would be covered in fuel. For part of my childhood I thought he was a mechanic of some sort. I knew he worked around trucks, and we went to visit his warehouse quite a few times. In fact, my aunt Valerie's boyfriend at the time, Alfonso, worked with him. Of course Pops pronounced his name Fonzie like on the show *Happy Days*. The fuel used to be so black he would use Ajax to wash up and get it off of him. One night Pops came in the house after work without Fonzie. He was whispering to my mom and aunts and didn't want us curious kids to hear him. Well, it turned out Pops used to siphon gas out of the trains that would dock near his warehouse. The train depot had finally gotten security. Pops was able to outrun them, but on this night Fonzie got caught. They had him arrested, and Pops and my aunt had to go to court and bail him out. He laughed after they were home, saying, "Why you young boys don't know how to run—how you go and get yourself caught?" That was the day we found out why Pops would always come home smelling like diesel fuel. Grandma would always make him leave his clothes in the bathroom. My cousins and I would always go sneak and watch Pops get cleaned up. We were always amazed because he used Ajax to wash his feet and hands, which confused us; we thought Ajax was used for cleaning the house. You know the way they joked in the movie *My Big Fat Greek Wedding*, "Windex for everything"? Well, my grandpa used Ajax for everything.

At one time my pops weighed nearly three hundred pounds, all solid muscle and no body fat—that's why he outran Fonzie (I say that laughing). He used to make a muscle in his arm and pull it real fast to make it look like a frog jumping. After my mother moved out, Pops would come up to our apartment just to have peace away from my grandma and because my mother would let him eat and drink as much as he wanted. He was so handsome, and he didn't care what we did as long as he was around us. I remember once Pops let me cut his hair. My mom had some clippers in the house and I said, "Pops, let me cut your hair." He said, "Timmy, do you know what you are doing?" and I said, "Yes, Pops. I do it to my Barbie head all the time." Needless to say I went too far back on the front of his head, so when I finished the hairline was nearly in the middle of his head. Everyone laughed at him, and I cried because I thought I was going to be in trouble. I thought for sure I would get a big butt-whooping. Pops looked in the mirror and said, "Come here, Timmy." I went to him and he said, "Why you crying? It looks nice." Awwww. That's what I loved about my pops; he ended up having to cut his hair bald, but he still told me I did a good job.

Times later became very hard, and Pops started losing weight rapidly. He would never, ever go to the hospital; like most men he did not like hospitals. Pops would be in pain and he never let us know anything; he never complained. My mother got together with my aunts and uncles and eventually made him go to the hospital. We were told that he had bone and lung cancer. I truly believe that all that diesel fuel had a lot to do with his developing cancer; coupled with cigarettes without the filters, it didn't help the fact that he worked around a lot of chemicals back when they did not have the proper protection to handle it. My granddad went from nearly 300 pounds to under 150 pounds. He was so light that my aunts were able to put him in bed.

That next year was the quietest the house would ever be. My grandmother didn't argue with him; she still didn't let him sleep in her bed, but she gave him peace. That was the first time I learned about the weight-gain shakes. We used to buy them for Pops by the case; he didn't eat much because he rarely had an appetite, and we were trying to maintain his weight.

Pops became really sick, and instead of going into the hospital for his final days he wanted to go home to his mother's house in South Carolina. When my pops left and said goodbye that was the last time I would ever see him. We didn't know he wasn't coming back, we just thought he was going to visit, but he knew and didn't want to be in the house where we could see him. He died in October 1987.

This is very hard for me to write, but you have got to let your loved ones know you love them; you have to hug them like you don't want to let go. As I'm typing these words, I can barely see the screen from my tears. My kids said I must be crying over a bad memory, but no, these were some of the happiest days of my life. I just hope that even though I was young and didn't always tell him how much he meant to me, my pops knew that he was my pops and I love him so much, I miss him so much. I can still hear him calling my name wrong, but calling it nonetheless.

I just thought of something my grandpop's nephew said that took me from crying to smiling. He told us that the day before my pops died Pops asked him for a cigarette and a drink. Of course his nephew told him, "You know the doctors won't let you have that." Well, after Pops died the nephew told us he was walking in the barn and it felt like something pushed him down. He said, "Stop, Uncle Nate, you know you couldn't have that drink," and then he felt a wind and it seemed like his uncle Nate was laughing at him for falling.

We didn't have money back in those days, so none of the grandkids were able to go to South Carolina for the funeral; only the children went. My grandmother didn't go. I think it was because 1. She felt guilty for the way she treated him, and 2. She thought his sisters would whoop her behind because of the way she treated him. The only thing she was really worried about was collecting spousal SSI. When God turns things around I want to go to South Carolina and visit my pops' grave. He was buried next to his mother and father.

Pops, thank you for showing me what a father really is. You took care of eight children back when you probably only made $100 per week. You never learned how to read or write, you never went past the third grade in school, but you learned how to take care of and work to feed your family.

Chapter 8

My First Love

～ン

Anthony was this five-foot-four, 130-pound, hazel-eyed, red-bone-fine-as-I-don't-know-what man. We first met when we both attended Dr. Martin Luther King Jr. High School on 66th Street and Amsterdam Avenue. Doug E. Fresh was a senior and we were all freshmen. After school we all rode the train uptown. Anthony had just come into the country from Belize and lived on 148th Street and St. Nicholas Avenue along with his mother and very tiny grandmother. Being from Belize, they looked Spanish but spoke Patwa (West Indian). Anthony was small in stature and had "little man" syndrome; he always had to be the one in control. The group of guys he hung out with stayed around him all the time as though they were his bodyguards; he never went anywhere alone.

I remember the first time I saw Anthony. He was with a couple of guys walking from Broadway towards Amsterdam coming right up 160th, and I was sitting on the outside stoop with Jimmy. Jimmy and I used to ride the train together because we both attended the same school and of course grew up around one another. When I saw Ant I looked at Jimmy and we both said to one another, "That's the guy from King." As I turned back in Ant's direction he was saying the same thing to his friend Harv, "That's Shorty from King." What I didn't know at the time was that he actually walked through the block on purpose because he was trying to find me. At the time, Ant's friend Harv was dating my friend Yo, which gave them an excuse to come around my way like they were looking for her. Yo lived in Queens. Eventually I let Yo and Harv hook the two of us up.

I was a virgin when I met Anthony. Yes, he was my first love and the first man I had ever slept with. I didn't have a clue as to what I was doing—obviously neither one of us did, because we didn't even use any protection. I had gone over to Anthony's grandma's one-bedroom apartment. Anthony slept on the sofa and there was a bedroom with two beds in it, one for his mother and the other for his grandmother. When he opened the door he had a raw steak on his face. I thought, Okay, this must be some kind of a joke. It turned out he was picked up the night before by the police, and I guess since he was always a step ahead of them they couldn't pin anything on him, so they beat him up instead of holding him under arrest. At that particular time I didn't know it was over drugs. Anthony didn't care; he was still a smart-mouth little bad ass. That was the same day I lost my virginity. I remember trying to be careful not to touch his eye; I was so scared it would hurt him. We slept on his grandma's bed and it hurt like I don't know what. It took us a few tries, and it was very weird because he just kept asking me was I okay, was he hurting me. Well yeah, it hurt, but we still wanted to be with each other. After it was all over he had relieved himself all over the covers. We tried to clean it up, but his grandma thought he'd been eating on her bed and spilled something, so we actually got away with it.

I was so in love with Anthony, but he had a dark side that I just could not see, at least not at first. For one thing, he was not faithful to me; he continued to carry on with lots of other women even when we were together. And then there was the drugs—but it took me a long time to catch on to that.

When I say I grew up in New York around drugs, it's truly no exaggeration. There was a girl arrested for carrying drugs on the Greyhound. Looking back, I'm sure she was set up and the police were tipped off. According to the parts of the story I heard, the police knew she was coming in with drugs. It was said that she was transporting the drugs across state lines from New York to Virginia. I do not know her name; I only know it was the sister of yet another female that Anthony messed around on me with. I believe her sister's name was Chante. Well, Chante's sister supposedly got arrested, and although the police were certain that she was Anthony's mule they could not prove it and she was not telling. These women would go to jail for Anthony before they would tell.

There was this one time when I was lucky not to get picked up for transporting drugs. Of course I didn't know anything about it at the time, but looking back I can understand what was going on. Anthony was living in Virginia back then, where he was supposedly running his family's jewelry business, and he and his cousin Darren (I don't believe Darren was his real cousin—that's just what Anthony called him) came to New York to visit. Darren brought his then-girlfriend with him. Yes, he met her in Norfolk straight out of the projects (when I first visited from New York I thought they were houses, but it turned out they were considered the projects and in a not-so-good neighborhood). I was going down to spend the weekend with Anthony, and since they were coming up I waited to go back with them. Darren's girlfriend went shopping and was spending a lot of money. I didn't think anything at the time. I knew she lived in the projects, but I figured Darren gave her the money since he was dating her. Nothing ever rang a bell. Once again when I met Anthony he told me that his family owned a jewelry store out of state, so whenever he had on new jewelry or he gave me presents I never thought twice about it; I assumed the store was in Virginia, which was why he moved there.

When we were leaving New York to go to Norfolk, Anthony and Darren caught an earlier flight. I can't remember why exactly; I thought it was because I still had school and my mom, although she gave me too much freedom in letting me travel to Virginia, wouldn't let me go during school time. Anyway, Darren's girlfriend and I flew down together, and we flew first-class—Anthony always had me fly first-class when I went to visit him.

When the plane landed we picked up the bags from baggage claim and walked out of the airport to take a taxi to their apartment. A little later Darren's girlfriend came over to me and was so nervous and scared. I had no idea why she was acting the way she was. I figured maybe she and Darren had gotten into an argument. She would not say anything to me even though I tried to ask, and when I mentioned it to Anthony he said, "Shorty, that b**** is dirty. F*** her. She know I don't f****** play that s***." Anthony would get like that sometimes, and whenever he would start his cussing I just said, "There goes that Creole coming out." He said, "Shorty, you are my woman; you don't carry nobody's bags. I don't give a f***." When we were leaving the airport Darren's girlfriend had so many bags because she'd just gone shopping, and since I only had a weekend bag I picked up some of her stuff to help her out. Then when Anthony saw me helping her at the apartment he flipped his lid. Of course this didn't make any sense to me at the time, but later, after everything started to come out, I put two and two together. I eventually learned about how women were being arrested for transporting drugs, and now I wonder if by carrying her bag I unwittingly helped this woman finish transporting something. Lord knows I didn't have a clue back then. Thank you, God, for covering and protecting me from the unknown.

It's strange how you can be with someone and not know the life they live. Even later, after all the charges came out, Anthony still denied everything to me. He would never let me know or be involved in that part of his life, but he did tell me how bad he was as a child growing up in Belize. He would just tell me he would never let me leave him, that he would kill me and bury me where no one would ever find my body.

Anthony told me how the big thing in Belize was when tourists went to visit. One day he robbed a female tourist for a diamond bracelet and money. He actually was caught by the police, but he still got away. They searched him and couldn't find anything on him to connect him to the robbery. Turns out this mastermind placed the bracelet in his underwear around his private area so when he was searched the police didn't find anything. All I could do was just look at him and say, "Can you ever stay out of trouble?"

Anthony was missing for over a week when he went to Belize to bring one of his sisters out. They had to hide and travel through the hills and across the border through Mexico. His mother and I were so worried because the man that was helping them cross had left them because the border patrol was too heavy. This man eventually did go back for the group he was bringing into the country. Anthony and his sister came walking into the house smiling and not worried at all, as though nothing had happened.

This man was always up to something, and it was usually something no good. One day I got a phone call from Norfolk, Virginia. This girl said, "Shanise, he just got arrested." I asked her who got arrested and she told me it was Anthony. I told her okay, I would fly down. So many things were going through my mind during the plane ride down from New York; I didn't know what to expect. By this time I was five or six months pregnant with my oldest daughter, Tiff. Darren's girlfriend met me at the airport and took me to her apartment for the night so that we could go to court in the morning. No one would say anything around me or to me in fear that Anthony would hurt them if they did.

When I arrived at the courtroom I met this attorney. I had no idea who he was, but he was representing Anthony. I later found out that in 1988 he was the best criminal attorney that money could buy in Virginia. Anthony later told me that his legal fees for the case totaled $40,000. So here I am sitting in a courtroom, pregnant and not knowing what's about to happen to this man, the love of my life. I watched them bring Anthony across the room. He was walking weird, taking very small steps, and I noticed he was walking with his hands cuffed and ankles shackled. A chain hung down connecting the handcuffs to the shackles. I didn't know what to think at this point. I still didn't know why we were there.

How could I have been so naïve? Everyone in the courtroom knew what was going on except me. I was numb, sitting there dazed just listening to charges being called out; it was as if I had fallen into a trance. I heard someone talking but didn't know where the voices were coming from. I heard multiple charges. Anthony was charged with being a pimp. The women were selling their bodies so they could get money to buy drugs; they were prostituting themselves. He was also charged with being a kingpin. Of course I had no idea what "kingpin" meant. The explanation was that Anthony was the "Godfather of Virginia," he had all of Norfolk under his reign, he was the leader of a drug ring that dealt in large quantities of kilos. The drug task force (DEA agents) took his picture to all the schools, telling children to be aware of him and to stay away from him, he was very bad news.

Anthony was all over the newspapers. According to the papers, he raked in hundreds of thousands of dollars. The judge remanded him without bail. I got up and nearly fainted. I just remember him calling out to me, "Shorty, it's going to be okay. Shorty, don't cry; you are going to hurt the baby." At the same time a couple of DEA agents were standing in front of me saying, "That's his wife," although Anthony and I were never married. I guess it was a first for the police to see me, just like it was a first for me to hear the charges.

I watched them take Anthony in shackles back into a white van with the name of the jail written on the sides. I was young, pregnant, about to have our child, and he was not going to be there.

I didn't know what to do. When my first child was born her father was in prison. In order for her to get his last name I had to fly down before I gave birth, hand a prison guard the parent form, and Anthony had to say, "Yes, this is my child; I want the baby to have my name." He told me he would be there for me and the baby, but he let us down. I do not know why, regardless of what he was doing, the prospect of becoming a father didn't make him stop before it reached this point. I was so angry and scared, and suddenly, at just eighteen years old, I had to do it all on my own.

My aunt Valerie was determined to go in the delivery room with me, but it still was not the same; Anthony was supposed to be there with me. Well, on August 24, 1988, I went into labor, and everything went according to plan. You see, my aunt wanted to go because she didn't have children yet and she wanted to see how it was going to be. Well, guess what? I picked the wrong aunt to go. When the pain started getting closer, my aunt left me in the room by myself. I was alone because she let my mother and other aunts go home; she was going to be there to help me. She left the delivery room and never told me why or where she went, but I think she went to puff some weed because when she went out she was a wreck, but when she came back in she was mellow and you could smell the marijuana scent coming off her clothes. Then all she kept saying was "Little Anthony is coming. Push little Anthony out." Now keep in mind that a woman in labor cannot maintain her kindness. Finally my head spun around and I looked at her and told her, "You have got to be kidding me. You are talking about a freaking jailbird. I don't want to push little Anthony out; he should be here and pull it out." I think by that time I was delirious and not making sense, and when it was all over Tiffanie was here, weighing 6 pounds 14 ounces. I thanked my aunt for being a trooper and hanging in there with me even though she left for a little while and at one point I became very ignorant.

Anthony was a very protective father, even from prison. He would call wanting to know who was around the baby, he didn't want me to take her outside, he didn't want anyone to come see her. When I first had Tiff and his friends came to see her, I thought, Okay, they want to see the baby. But Anthony got furious when he found out. He told me, "I don't want no f****** body going to see you or my kid." He drove me nuts. I told him it was just his friends and he said, "Shorty, listen to me. I'm going to tell them niggers they better stay away from y'all." I just let him talk, thinking that he couldn't do anything anyway. I just kept throwing it back in his face that he was not there and he made me go through it by myself. I was really surprised by the way he was acting but didn't understand at the time that he was trying to protect us; he didn't want anyone knowing where we were just in case they wanted to hurt us to get back at him. Thank God for covering us, because I really didn't have a clue back then.

The only person that Anthony would trust around me and the baby was Sam, one of his right-hand men. Sam always gave me money for Tiff so that I could get diapers and clothes while Anthony was in jail. He and his brother Mark were part of the group of best buddies around Anthony. They were all good-looking, very handsome guys. All they would do was smoke blunts all day long—you know, the weed inside the cigar paper. Sam, sad to say, was murdered, shot dead outside of a nightclub. It was said the killer was a guy Sam had beaten badly in a fight a few weeks earlier. Sam was drunk and most likely high off blunts the night he was shot, so he was caught off guard coming out of the nightclub and was unable to defend himself. That was a really dark time in Anthony's life, being in jail when one of his best friends was murdered. Everyone went to Sam's funeral. There was a famous rapper who was close to Sam from their childhood school days, and even he was there.

I took Tiff to the prison so that Anthony could see her for the first time. When he did he cried. Because I was from out of town I was allowed more than one visit and a private one also. He saw his daughter for the first time from behind a glass window. But the kicker was while we were visiting there was another girl there that was pregnant. I didn't know she was there to see Anthony because he never acknowledged her; he looked directly at me and Tiff. This woman was standing behind me the entire time; it was weird. As visiting hours were about to end and I was walking out to go see about a second visit, she got bold and went up to the window and told him, "Now you act like you don't know me." Something turned me around. When I saw her talking to him I went back up to him and I asked Anthony who this woman was, and he told her, "Don't f****** play with me. Don't you see me here with my wife and my daughter? Get the f*** out of here." By this time I lost it. I cussed him out and walked off. He was begging me to call him back out so he could explain it to me. Well, I never called him back out and I never again went to visit him in prison.

It turned out that this woman had a little boy and named him after Anthony—of course only the first name. He slept with so many women; everyone that knew what he was (his status as the head of the crew) and what he had in terms of money wanted to be with him. Anthony's sister and I could not get along, so she would encourage it. She was friends with all of the other girls he messed around with and those who liked him and would also bring this baby to visit in New York. I never knew of course, and Anthony wouldn't tell me until one time I went over to visit him in Brooklyn with Tiff and the boy was in the room. I had no idea until Anthony and his sister got into a big argument over it. Anthony came out of the room and told me we were leaving. Well, to make a long story short, his sister was best friends with this girl, and now that Anthony is deceased she just recently said she thinks Tiff and Britt are the only kids that actually belong to Anthony. She said there was another guy saying he was the little boy's father. The same girl that cheated with Anthony also cheated with her child's father and had a child. Be careful what you wish for, because what you intend for me God can turn it around for my good. What goes around comes around. Now she was able to feel the same hurt that I felt at the hands of the same woman. For me and the way I am seen in the eyes of God, I found it in my heart to forgive her.

I really was on my own at that time, left to raise Tiff with no real support from Anthony's family. They used to spend his money, at least what they were holding for him. They would always tell him that I needed money for the baby and that they gave me money for doctor's visits. They lied. Of course he never mentioned it to me as it was happening; that was much later. At least if he had, I would have been able to tell him it was a lie. Although his mother was there emotionally, she never once gave the kids money. I remember one time she said she bought Tiff some diamond earrings; well, we never got them. There was another time she told me she bought Tiff some bracelets from Belize (red gold); well, again we never got them. There would be times during birthdays that she would say she bought a gift and would send it to us. Well, again we never once received any birthday or Christmas gifts. By this time I was so mad at her I stopped taking Tiff to see her. I felt that they were the reason Anthony was not stopping what he was doing. I blamed his mother for not trying harder to make him stop. After he had become angry when he found out about the lies, his mother then decided to talk with me. She told me about an incident that happened one afternoon during school hours when Anthony and I were both still in high school. Ant and one of his friends had just gotten in from Virginia and were walking through Times Square when the police picked them up for truancy (skipping school). Keep in mind Ant looked very young for his age. The police took them into the subway precinct and held them there until Ant's mother came down to pick them up. Ant had over $50,000 in his backpack, but the police never searched their bags. Since they considered it a simple truancy, they most likely assumed the boys were carrying books during school hours. Bottom line was she was never the one to blame; Anthony always could have stopped and made a life for us. Me, him, and Tiff.

I was with a drug dealer. Young women need to watch out for this. The mere fact that I didn't know everything that was going on at the time doesn't make it right, and being ignorant of the fact that your man is cheating on you doesn't make it hurt any less. To have women say they were pregnant with Anthony's child meant he had unprotected sex with them and put me and our girls in a dangerous position. He could have given us AIDS. I was eighteen years old, pregnant with my first child, and during one of my visits to the midwife I found out Anthony had given me an STD (thank God he didn't give me AIDS). It could be cured in my case, but the treatment took longer for me since I was pregnant and couldn't take the normal dose of medication. Three times a day I had to take these tablets that looked like something a veterinarian would give to a horse. My child was also at risk, and thank God she was covered from being born blind. Young women, you can't afford to be as naïve as I was; keep your eyes open, know what you're getting into, and if something doesn't feel right, you need to walk away.

Anthony and I had separated for a while. With all that had gone on, I never graduated from high school. I dropped out and took my GED, but I scored so high on it that I was actually given a high school diploma. Suddenly college and law school didn't look like such a possibility. I was a young, single mother who never walked across the stage at my high school graduation; I never even got to go to my high school prom with the rest of my friends. That made me perfect welfare material, right? Now I could sit back, talk about how hard life was, and collect a check from the government, right? Wrong. That generational curse was going to be broken, and I still knew I would be the one to break it. So what did I do? I went on with my life, still staying with my mother, and got a job working at the courthouse as a clerk for the legal aid society. That was one of the hardest jobs I have ever held in my life. It was both good and a very bad evil. It was good that we were helping the children get out of abusive homes. The bad part was that I saw cases where fathers would molest their own children or crackhead mothers would sell their babies. I had benefits and health insurance for me and Tiff. My life was going good. There were two things I could never get over though. First, the horrors I'd witnessed made it so hard for me to leave my children with anyone; I didn't trust anybody. Second, I could never get over Ant; he was the love of my life, and whenever he came to see Tiff I could see the hurt in his face when she had to go to bed and he had to leave. Tiff was his heart; she was Daddy's little girl. So, in order to be Tiff's father, Anthony finally straightened up and got over the drug life.

Tiff was a little over two years old when I found out I was pregnant again. This time Anthony promised to be there with me so I didn't have to go through it without him. August 29, 1991, was the night I went into labor. I had to call him because he was staying with his mother in Brooklyn. He caught a ride to the hospital on the back of a motorcycle; this was at the end of August, so I know the ride had to be pretty cold. Britt came very fast. Anthony barely made it to the hospital. I was on a bed in the hallway looking out the window facing the George Washington Bridge. It was early morning so you could see the beautiful lights still on. The hospital was crowded, and even though they were trying to prepare my room, Britt was not waiting, she was preparing to enter the world. The doctors put up a partition around me and just started taking the bed apart, when next thing I knew they were telling me to push. Anthony was standing behind me holding me up and telling me to push. He was doing good, until he made the mistake of trying to see what was going on in front of us. When he saw the baby's head crowning and all the blood, this tough man passed out on the floor. So Anthony was there, but I had to do it without him once again. After it was all done we laughed so hard talking about how he got woozy and we had to get him some crackers. Brittney was born weighing 7 pounds 4 ounces.

Here I was, twenty-one years old, having just given birth to our second child. I still really didn't know what new line of work Anthony was into. At the time I didn't realize how he protected us, me and the girls, from it.

You know Anthony really did think he was Scarface, Tony Montana. He would wear nothing but the finest clothes. He built a home in Belize that he told me had a pool on the roof. Back in 1988 before all the rappers were wearing all these diamonds on their teeth, he was the very first person I ever saw with it. He had a row of gold teeth—three teeth had rubies and the other three had diamonds in them. His famous footwear was Bally, and all of his clothes would be custom made. Anthony would give me anything I wanted, oftentimes just showing up with something for me that he wanted me to have. Despite all the bad things that he did, I could only remember how good he was to me. Back then I didn't know any better. In reality I was in a controlling relationship. Anthony controlled my every move, my surroundings—he even controlled what I could know about him.

Anthony used to always threaten me to keep me from leaving him. Once again his famous words were "If you leave me I will kill you and bury you where no one would find your body." Sadly, and naïvely, I took him as joking, but this was something he was actually capable of doing at any time.

The way he kept things from me, the numerous young ladies that I hear he was their first love too. How could he and why would he do this to me? Did Anthony really think that, as long as I was what he considered his main girl, the mother of his kids, it hurt me any less? Did he really think it was all okay as long as these other women knew about me and I didn't know about them? I received a prank telephone call one day. The caller said, "Why are you still with him? Why did you take him back? He gave you an infection and you still took him back." This call came from someone that knew Anthony had given me that STD infection. You would think that this, on top of everything else, would be enough to make me leave, but my twisted mind back then told me if I left Anthony he would be with these other women, and I didn't want that to happen. Also, no one realized that he was not letting me leave.

I finally got away from Anthony, but I didn't realize that it was because he knew he was in trouble and was leaving, evading the police, and he wasn't coming back. He may have protected us from the criminal activities, but he only cared about himself when he left to flee to his hometown in Belize. However, trouble followed him.

I sit here now, and as much as it pains me and as cruel as it sounds, his being wanted by the FBI and fleeing was the best thing for me and my girls. There's no telling what would be going on with us or where the girls and I might have ended up. I did eventually realize that Anthony and all these young, good-looking dudes were ruthless. They were into some serious stuff, charges ranging from kingpin to prostitution—so many charges—and my sweet Ant, the smallest out of the group, was considered the mastermind. Imagine he was the ringleader and I was his kids' mother. I chose to believe that he left us so that he could protect us.

He said he was going to Belize to visit his father who was sick and, may he rest in peace, later died. Anthony never came back, though. What I didn't know was that he actually could not come back to the states because of a bank robbery he'd committed; he and all the guys involved fled to Belize. That was another thing I didn't learn the whole truth about until much later.

At first I used to speak with him a lot, but that changed after the death of his father. After losing all contact with Anthony for almost a year and a half, out of the blue one day I was talking on the telephone to his sister Karen in Belize. I had not spoken to her since she was deported from the states. I sent her pictures of the girls, we spoke about the girls and the family, and she told me how Anthony would brag to the people in Belize that I was a good mother and how the girls had everything and didn't want for anything. She told me how he was heartbroken and very upset with me that I went and got married. About two or three weeks after that, one day I received a telephone call from a young lady saying she was calling me on behalf of Anthony's family, she was a family friend. I never got her name, and to this day I do not know who she was. The caller said, "Anthony is dead," and that was it. About a day passed, and after finally getting a hold of his mother, I was told that Anthony was murdered on November 30, 1997. Turns out, his mother told me this group of guys that he used to hang out with were sitting in a bar planning to rob and kill him. The bartender overheard this and went over to the house to warn Anthony, but when he got there Karen, Anthony's sister, said her brother was not there, he'd gone out with the guys. The bartender told Karen, "Oh no, I'm too late." He told her the plans he'd overheard. Anthony's car was found abandoned in the woods with his bloodied shirt inside. His body was never recovered and the men were never charged with anything. The family thought that he was thrown into the alligator-infested bayou. Twelve years later they still have not found his remains and no one has been charged with his murder. Ironically, this is the exact same death that Anthony used to threaten me with. I am now a believer in not taking a person's comments to you lightly, especially if it's in the form of a threat.

His mother had asked me to let the girls go to Belize for Anthony's memorial, but I refused. Aside from the fact that his body was not recovered, I didn't know what might happen if those guys came to the memorial, so I put my children's safety first.

Anthony's mother had a nervous breakdown after the murder. People thought I would be the one to have a breakdown, but in my heart there is no closure for me. It was actually up to my daughter Britt to find out why he was really back in Belize in the first place and why he couldn't return to the states. She decided to do some research on her father and found the entire case since it is public record. The things we read were astounding. Anthony's sister Karen testified against him at trial. She was the witness for the state. When she was originally interviewed by the FBI, Karen claimed that Anthony was not even her brother. Her testimony may not have been totally trustworthy, but she still had a lot to say. She testified that Anthony and his friend Kelroy planned this robbery in Virginia. They had masks to wear during the robbery and drove to the bank in a stolen car. At the bank, Kelroy collected the money while Anthony held a gun on the tellers. They had it all planned out, even ditching the getaway car and riding in another accomplice's trunk and arranging for someone to burn their clothes. Then they fled, first to North Carolina, then to New York and eventually Belize. Kelroy was later convicted of unarmed bank robbery and conspiracy to commit bank robbery. Who knows what would have happened to Anthony if he had come back to the states?

I pray for my girls to have peace over the loss of their father. It took me a very long time to get over him. He was my first love, and I have always loved him, but the reality is he was not some innocent great guy; he ruined lives. Anthony may have taken care of us, but we were constantly in harm's way, and he was constantly bringing harm to others. Think of all those girls he was involved with when he had no intention of leaving us to be with them, and who knows how many households were destroyed because of the drugs? I can't paint Anthony as a good guy. He was good to me for a while after he decided to calm down, but that was before he got involved with that last group of guys, the bank robbers. This man led a double life and I had no clue. He was so very good at what he did that I never knew any of it. Anthony even has an FBI record for bank robbery that I never knew about. I now realize that to protect me and the girls he could not let me know anything. I was sleeping with and had children with a man that was a total stranger to me. So good and sweet to us, but ruthless and cold-blooded to others.

To this day I wonder where all of his money and jewelry went. The kids only received one piece of jewelry—Tiffanie got her father's name ring. He had thousands of dollars, he had diamonds, gold, and according to the police reports he made a lot of illegal money. When Anthony left the country he cared only about himself and not getting caught; he did not leave me with any money to help with the care of the children. I became a single mother with no source of additional income, and upon his death I was unable to collect social security for the children because Anthony never worked a legitimate job. I am sure it all went once again to the same one that spent his money when he was alive.

Chapter 9

Tornadoes

⟿

I have been told so many times by so many different people that I look like Jada Pinkett Smith. One of my favorite all-time movies was *A Low Down Dirty Shame*. My family would watch that movie over and over, always role-playing along with the film. The funniest character of them all was Wayman. He would roll his eyes and snap that head around. Ms. Jada was the sassy one—gorgeous, petite, strong willed, and just downright sassy. People always say one of these two things: I either look Ethiopian or I remind them of Jada. Since I have moved to Maryland and Jada is from Baltimore I get it even more now. I always said that when my life story comes out I want Jada Pinkett Smith to play me. I think it would be quite a role for her, considering all the things my life has taken me through.

I was married in New York on June 11, 1994. My father performed the ceremony. He'd been ordained as a minister in the early '90s, although I only remember seeing him go to church maybe three or four times in my whole life. Duke and I always argued, but never in front of the kids—I made sure of that. Because our two heritages were so different—he is Dominican and I'm American—we were bound to clash. There is a real difference in treatment of men and women between the two cultures. Dominican men are particularly spoiled by the women in their families, be it sisters or mothers, and I could never meet Duke's expectations of me.

The weekend after we got married we moved all the way to Atlanta, Georgia. I knew I had to finally move out of my mother's place since we were getting married, so I thought, Why not a new start in a new state? We moved into an apartment complex in Kennesaw and lived in an apartment that had a greenhouse. This meant my entire living room area had a glass ceiling. I'd never seen an apartment like that back in New York, so when I went inside I immediately fell in love with it and rented it. The only problem was that I never really researched Georgia before moving there. Needless to say, I didn't know the area was famous for tornadoes.

We didn't have much beyond the basic necessities when we moved. One night not too long after we got settled in, we were in the living room watching TV and it was raining very hard out. If you looked up you could see the trees blowing hard back and forth past the window. For hours we heard this horn blowing and blowing. We just said, "It's raining; let's turn off the TV and go to sleep." We all ended up sleeping in the living room. Duke and I were on the sofa and Tiff and Britt were on the loveseat. The next day we drove over to see my aunt Sue, who lived about fifteen minutes away in Marietta. She asked how we did with the storm, and I said, "The rain was okay; it's just that a horn kept blowing all night long." Aunt Sue told us that was a siren warning everyone that a tornado was coming. When you hear that horn, you're supposed to get away from all the windows, go into a bathroom, and get in the tub if you have to. Well, no one ever told us all that, so we actually did the complete opposite: We slept right under all the windows. Thank God for covering us back then. That was the first of many tornado warnings. Every year there would be at least five tornadoes. The last one that hit before we left Georgia was a category five, the strongest tornado possible. We were renting a townhouse in Doraville when that one hit. It killed a few people and knocked large trees down on top of houses. It even tore the roofs off of a couple of townhomes in the neighborhood. That was terrible and another of many parts of Georgia I do not miss.

One Fourth of July we were all sitting inside the house and heard a pop and then a big bang. I thought it was someone lighting firecrackers. A few minutes later, one of the neighbors knocked on the front door. I looked out the window because I was up in the girls' room, and I saw my Acura Legend with glass next to it. Brittney loved this car; she called it the Batman car. It was a navy blue coupe with the spoiler and the sun visor on top. Britt would always say, "Moms, are we going in the Batman car?" Well, getting back.... I went out to the front door, and the neighbor told me my car was hit. I said, "What?" We went outside to see the car, and it was smashed up, totaled, but there was nothing next to it. It turned out that there was a domestic dispute down the hill from where we lived. The wife and the kids had moved in with a new man. The husband apparently was crazy and would always harass the couple. Things escalated to the point he called the couple and told them that he was going over to kill them. When the husband got there they took it as another light threat, only this time the husband had a gun and he really was going to kill them. They managed to get the gun away from him and then shot him with his own gun (that was the pop we heard). The husband got into his car to drive off. He made it up the hill, but as he reached my car he passed out and ran smack into it—hit it so hard his car ended up on the other side of the street. The police rushed the man to the hospital, but he died before he arrived. The car was material, but I could never imagine the emotional trauma of that man's kids being there to see that.

Amber and J were both born while I lived in that townhouse. My marriage was rough, but I stayed. My husband was the type of person that didn't care if things were paid or not. I would often have to get my family to send us money. Georgia was not like New York, where people lived in their places for months without payment and would not be evicted.

One time before J was born the rent was only late by fifteen days. I didn't know that by the sixth of the month the management office would file evictions with the courts. I had already asked my family for the money because once again Duke didn't pay the rent nor did he try all means to get it. Uncle Tony, my mom, and Aunt Ann put the money together and sent it to me Western Union. The mistake I made was in not going to court because I knew I was going to get the money to pay the rent and my brilliant husband told me they couldn't evict you until thirty days past due.

Well, the morning that I was going to the Western Union we had a knock at the front door. It was the sheriff and a bunch of guys there to remove our things and dump them at the front of the complex. I told them I had the money but needed to wait until Western Union opened to get it. The people in the leasing office were kind; I guess they realized it was an honest mistake and I really didn't know. They had a lot of evictions to do that day, so the lady in the office told them to go ahead with the others and come back to us last. I had less than an hour to put the money into their hands and they really didn't have to accept it. I called my mom and was crying, telling her they were at the door to put us out. She told me to go to the Western Union and that's what I did. I came back with the money and took it straight to the leasing office. Thank God the manager accepted it.

Duke had stayed in the house with the kids. When I opened the front door I saw stuff thrown all over the place. They were trying to gather up clothes for the kids before the sheriff came back to put us out. I grabbed my kids and hugged them so tight and kept saying, "I'm sorry. I'm sorry this had to happen. I'm sorry you saw this. I'm sorry you were scared." They were crying and saying, "I want Grandma!" They wanted to leave Georgia and move back to New York with my mom.

I called my mother back. My aunt, uncle, the entire family was at my mother's by then. They cussed my husband out and told me how he was not a man and didn't care about anyone but himself. They never saw me live like that before and told me not to let his no-good ass take me and the kids down; we were better than that. They also told me to come back home.

I stayed with Duke a little bit longer, but by this time his family had moved down. We fought because I didn't want them to move in with us; we only had a two-bedroom. I also found out he took our rent money and gave it to them. I didn't have anything to leave with; I had just gotten laid off because the company I was working for closed down. And not only had I just paid the rent, it was the middle of the month and rent would soon be due again. I went and spoke with a lawyer, thinking it would be a very easy divorce since we didn't have anything.

I hadn't grown up in any church, and to my knowledge no one in my family even attended church (except for those few times I remember my father going), so I really had no idea what God and the church were all about. One thing I did know was that I was broken and very unhappy. I had three daughters (my third daughter, Amber, was born on March 16, 1995, weighing in at 7 pounds 4 ounces; she was such a terror and a sweetheart all in one—her "terrible two" stage went well past two years old) and was pregnant with my son, and there I was living with a husband I couldn't even talk to.

Then one day I was watching television and a church service from Gospel Tabernacle came on. I watched their services on television for several weeks until I finally decided the kids and I were going to go. Now, I never did have a great sense of direction, and of course I got lost on the way to church. We'd been lost for almost an hour, and I was ready to give up and go home to watch church on TV again, but God took control. All of a sudden, there was the exit I'd been looking for. At the time I thought it was just dumb luck that I eventually found my way, but now I know better. God had a different plan for me, and he got me to that church on that day so I could hear the message he'd sent for me. That very day I answered the altar call and Bishop Wiley Jackson (he was Pastor Wiley Jackson at that time) prayed with me. It was incredible—I felt this great weight being lifted from me, and at the same time my body became so heavy I fell down. I surrendered it all to God and was overcome by the Holy Spirit. A few months later, on October 4, 1998, when I was about three months pregnant with my son and fourth child, I was baptized. It was the same day my daughters were all dedicated to Christ. I'll never forget it. Pastor Wiley had sons of his own, and when we walked up to the altar he joked that someone better go get his boys out of children's church so they could meet my beautiful daughters.

We continued to attend Gospel Tabernacle as long as we lived in Georgia. My kids went to their first Easter egg hunt there. Someday I will go back to visit now Bishop Wiley Jackson of "Word In Action" and see the new cathedral that was being built just as we were moving to Maryland.

But I need to backtrack a little bit now; there was some more stuff I had to go through with my husband before I would be able to leave. As I said, money was tight, and I had to go to the churches in Georgia and the Catholic Women's Center to ask for utility assistance and for help to pay the rent. I went to about five places. Most of them gave me their max of $100, and one gave me the max of $75. Finally the Catholic Women's Center helped me pay the rent, but first they sent two nuns to the house to minister to me about God. And my good-for-nothing husband wouldn't even go into the dining room to listen to what these two kind, sweet, old ladies that were about to pay our next month's rent had to say. I was very fortunate God still placed it in their hearts to help me and the kids. They wrote me a check for $750.

I called my family and was ready to go. But then I received a call from my attorney saying that my divorce case was being dismissed. It was 1998, I was pregnant with Jesurun, and in the state of Georgia you could not get a divorce while you were pregnant. The judge dismissed the case without even bothering to have a conversation with me. I had to wait until J was born and go back and file it again. Child support had to be agreed on before a divorce would be issued. We were able to get Amber's amount of $550 in place, but I was still pregnant with J. I received Amber's order and never looked back to ask for an increase once J was born.

One day in 1999 I was home with the kids when I got a phone call from Willie, my husband's nephew, saying that Duke was at work and had gotten locked up. I said, "Okay, where is he?" Now the first thing that came to my mind was he got into a fight with someone at work and they locked them up. Willie had to drive home the BMW 5 series that we had just purchased a few months before. He brought the car to my house, and then I drove him over to the apartment where they all stayed in Marietta, a nice expensive neighborhood. I could not imagine how they were able to afford this place and all the best furniture inside it. I went into the house and everyone was so secretive. His niece Courtney asked if she could go with me to the jail. She was the only honest one; she wanted to go so that she could tell me what was going on. This is when I found out that my husband was stealing from his job. He'd been arrested by his employer and charged with theft by deception, which is all public record.

So there I was, pregnant and about to give birth, and yet another man was in jail. Wow, here we go again. The charge was that he was allegedly making up false time cards with people that actually did not work at the company. After they cashed the checks Duke would get part of the money. There were a couple of other guys in on it with him, but they were never caught because they did not let greed get the best of them. I went to the jail and talked to Duke through the glass. He told me he did it and I asked him why. He surely was not using that money to support us. Before I went home I told him I was not trying to get any money to bail him out because I didn't help him get put in jail in the first place.

I couldn't take calls from him because they were collect. I did at first. When you pick up the phone you hear "Collect call for inmate at county jail. Will you accept?" But Duke started to call too much and wanted to be on the telephone a lot. I knew I had no way of paying that bill, so I had to let them place restrictions on letting the jail calls through.

Late one night I heard someone coming through the front door. I got up to see what was going on, and it was Duke. One of his friends put up his house for collateral so that Duke could get out of jail. Needless to say, they hadn't been friends very long for him to do something like that.

The next couple of months were tough. I finally had Jesurun, and the way our marriage was going I knew right then it could not be salvaged. I decided to take the kids and leave Georgia when J was just two months old. My father offered to let us stay in his house in Maryland rather than going all the way to New York. I never went back to the divorce court in Georgia because I knew I could do it in Maryland.

Well, my ex and I went back and forth for months. He tried to get me to move back to Georgia. I didn't have an address for where he was living, and while I wanted to file divorce papers months turned into years. Then on February 21, 2002, I was served divorced papers at work. I kept trying to find him to serve him with papers, but then he went and filed the divorce against me. This was another marathon for no reason at all.

The kids and I had been living in Maryland since July of 1999. In the petition my ex asked me for alimony and child support. He actually said the kids lived with him and he wanted me to pay him child support. This amounted to him perjuring himself on the record, and when I issued all of the kids' doctors' records and school records his attorney withdrew from the case around April 2002.

You would have thought it would be simple, but it became even more complicated. The judge on the case became furious with me and called me from inside her chambers to let me know that I had to show up in court and couldn't try a case over the phone long distance. She gave him joint custody of the kids based on the divorce document where he'd perjured himself by stating he had custody of the kids, leaving the judge under the assumption that the kids and I resided in Georgia. Well, by this time I'm thinking I have to give everything up and go on the run with my kids because there was no way I would let this man take my kids. The judge would not hear any other argument. I had to spend $15,000 on an attorney and finally, on July 23, 2003, appeal the case in the higher court.

I did fly down to Georgia to go before the judge. All the attorneys spoke about this judge and said she didn't overturn any decisions. In order to do that, she had to also acknowledge that her initial ruling was a mistake. I didn't care if she admitted it or not; all I wanted to hear was that she was not going to take my kids and give them to him. God was on our side. Maryland got jurisdiction over the kids, and Georgia got jurisdiction over the divorce. The judge tried to make me out to be a bully. My ex showed up without a lawyer and in clothes that didn't even fit him, and I had this high-powered divorce lawyer next to me. He actually had the nerve to come up to me to say hello and act like he was glad to see me. I wasn't truly saved back then and told him to go to hell. Obviously the whole church thing hadn't quite taken hold in me yet.

I did eventually forgive Duke, and I had a lot to forgive. The biggest thing that came to my mind was when I was pregnant with J, I remember being in the bathroom crying my eyes out because Duke did not support the pregnancy; he made it clear by his actions. He was very mean and turned into a nasty individual who wouldn't help me with anything. Until this day he still hates me, and sadly, although we have children together he doesn't know how to speak to me in a respectful way, which is why all communication between him and me has been severed. He saw his son Jesurun for the first time since he was two months old at my daughter Shavonna's high school graduation party. That particular night I thought would be a change for the better and that he would want to continue being a part of the children's lives. Well, it didn't happen; he went right back to being the stranger.

Just recently Jesurun had to call his uncle P-nut so that he could do his homework on his family tree. He called P-nut to ask all about his paternal side, and the saddest part is when I heard him ask for Duke's father's name. My son never even met his paternal grandfather. And he called his dad by his first name, Julio, because he never knew his father. Aside from the kids' sister Shavonna, P-nut and his wife and children have been the only relatives from their father's side that have ever tried to be a part of the kids' lives and have contact with them on a regular basis.

As I said before, after meeting Jesurun that one time Duke never continued the contact with them. Amber doesn't consider him her father. She calls him by his first name whenever anyone talks about him. I have been speaking to her about forgiveness so that she doesn't carry this hurt around with her. I pray every day for my children to have peace in their hearts.

Another thing I would like to add is that my ex-husband was in a relationship with a woman with five children. What he didn't understand was living in a household and paying for food, paying rent, paying the light and telephone bill was taking care of someone else's children. I would never have a problem with that if he were making any effort to also take care of his own children. But Duke never sent Christmas gifts, birthday cards, nothing to Amber and Jesurun. He wouldn't even go into a Dollar Store to pick up a gift. That really pissed me off until I was able to forgive him. I never forgot the way he has treated my children, but that is something he will have to stand before God to answer for. Truly I feel very sorry for him. He missed out on so many wonderful things happening in the lives of a couple of wonderful children.

Sometimes when you are in an abusive relationship, a person on the outside tries to talk with you to help you—they say they can see something is wrong, but you do not believe them because you think they are lying. Again, although I was not in a physically abusive relationship, I was being mentally abused. As I sit down now with my family and look back at old family movies and pictures, I can't recognize myself. During my marriage I aged about fifteen years. I looked so miserable, so much older than I really was, so insecure. I'd let myself go, I was not myself. Today when I look into the mirror I love who I see because I am able to stand strong and show my children a role model; I can give them a sense of normalcy. I look much younger than I am, I am beautiful, I keep myself up, I have God in my life, I am secure, confident, and I walk around with the boldness of Jesus on me. I look at my ex and, after seeing the way he treats his children, the way he acted towards me with such hate, the lies and the dragged-out divorce, I feel sorry for him. I forgive him but really feel sorry for him. Again, I don't have the right to judge him because he will stand before God and answer to God only, but I look a hundred times better than he does, even with being a single mother raising four children on my own.

People in these relationships make excuses, get scared of change, get comfortable in a bad situation, think things wouldn't be better if they left. I know because I've been there, but I am here to tell you it's the opposite. Things can only get worse the longer you stay; you start to lose track of who you were before the relationship. I myself completely forgot how beautiful and fun life was. I have made many mistakes with different men since I left my ex-husband, but I am not afraid to try. No, things haven't always been perfect. We get used to that same type of guy and make the mistake of picking more not-so-good-for-you guys. You will weed through them just as I did. I am experiencing life now, and if you trust God the same as I do, then you will know that God has someone out there to love you for you, someone to treat you with the respect and decency you need to be treated with and to be your partner and help you get through situations.

You will even establish new friendships. When I first married my ex, my daughter Shavonna's mother and I could not get along. Until we both got past the hurts Duke dealt to both of us, it was hard to hold a civil conversation. However, we had one common denominator: a deadbeat father. It was like pulling teeth and nails to get him to help her out with Shavonna, which should have been no surprise when he didn't want to help Amby and J either. Well, there is strength in numbers, and as single mothers Darlene and I have become very good friends. Our children are siblings and will always spend as much time together as they possibly can. The two of us were set on making sure they all would experience the best of times. When Shavonna graduated high school Duke told Darlene he would help her out with the party and other things; well, of course he personally did not come through. I got a phone call from my daughter telling me she didn't have enough money for her prom, and immediately I got on the phone with her mom and sent them money. It was such a joy when I received her prom pictures. Vice versa, when we did the fundraiser to send Britt to Australia to run track (which you will read about in later chapters), Darlene called me, asked for the bank account number the fundraiser was under, and she went and made a deposit, helping Britt have an experience of a lifetime.

I pray for all of you who are currently in the position I once was in that you just trust God and carefully remove yourself from your current situation. I am no expert, but there are organizations available to help you. I thank God for the help of my family. Things really can be better.

Chapter 10

Uncle Tony

I am very fortunate to have had a strong male role model in my life, aside from my grandfather, and that is Tony, my Uncles. This is the man who showed me what a real father is like. Some men won't even love and take care of their own children, as I learned very well from my father. Then there are those special men, like my uncle, who will shower love and caring on children who aren't even theirs.

Back when we were young, Uncles (as all of his nieces call him) was this skinny, nerdy kid who wore Steve Urkel glasses. Uncles may have looked wimpy, but he wasn't. He'd stand up to anyone who messed with his family, no matter how big the bully was. He's our protector even now, but he isn't a skinny little kid anymore. Now Uncles is a very buff man without an ounce of body fat—a far cry from his former Urkel image.

Once when I lived in Georgia, Uncles came down to visit us and caused a bit of a stir at the mall. People thought he was Dwayne Wayne from the TV show *A Different World*. Of course he played it up, letting all the girls get their pictures taken with him. It was hilarious!

My Uncles is a lot of fun, but what I really love him for is the way he's always there when we need him. He's such a blessing to me and to my kids in the way he looks out for us, and especially in the way he models manly behavior. At different times he's made sure the kids and I would have a roof over our heads, and once when I needed money and Uncles didn't have any to give me, he went and borrowed from someone just so he could help me. If my kids needed something, Uncles would make sure they got it. All that, *and* he would step in to babysit whenever needed. Now that is a real man!

Chapter 11

My Start in the Car Business

～

I dedicate this chapter to my very good friend Rebecca Richardson living with MS—Multiple Sclerosis.

One really good thing to come out of my time in Georgia was my early career in the car business. My original plan to become a lawyer hadn't worked out, but that didn't mean I couldn't still enjoy a challenging, lucrative career, as I would soon find out. I didn't need a fancy college degree to succeed; instead I could get on-the-job training and steadily work my way up. I wasn't even aware of all the possibilities back in 1994, when I first got into the car business with a job as a loan clerk making around twenty-one thousand a year. The company I worked for was called DAC Corporation. They would do high-interest loans on older-model cars. An "older model" was considered anything at least seven years from the current year, meaning they financed 1987 models and up. This is where I met my friend Sandy who, if I remember correctly, worked in the accounting department. Sandy was a young lady, strong willed and with a prior military background. We used to have a lot of fun together.

Sandy never liked my husband. She knew he was good for nothing and would always tell me I could do better. I remember she was furious the time our lights were turned off. She came to the house, got me and the kids, and took us to her apartment. She said I should just leave his a** there with his sorry self. Sandy always said she would help me and the kids but not my husband.

At one time I used to envy Sandy. She had separated from her husband and was single with no kids. She could buy what she wanted and come and go as she pleased. Then, after she and I talked, I realized Sandy felt the same way about me. She envied me because I wasn't alone; I had good beautiful kids that would show me love.

We worked together at DAC for about a year before I went on maternity leave because I had just given birth to Amber. It was during that time the company went out of business. Sandy and I remained friends though, but I am sorry to say that I lost touch with her when I moved to Maryland.

After giving birth to Amber, I went to work for ACC, where I made another close friend in the business. I didn't know it at the time, but the manager had hired me to replace Rebecca. The manager never really cared much for her, probably because she knew more about the car business than he did. Rebecca was also very close with the company's owners; she knew their wives, kids— Rebecca even knew their dogs' names.

Rebecca was the first black female employee at ACC, which had its corporate office in Long Beach. With a name like Rebecca Richardson no one knew she was black. The company was made up of Italians, Hispanics, and Greeks. With the right hair color Rebecca could easily pass for Hispanic or Greek. She sometimes dealt with racism on the job, but Rebecca was from the south, so that was nothing new to her. She knew exactly how to handle it, and would always say you should have a back-up plan, keep good notes, and document everything—you never know who's out to get you.

When Rebecca and I first met I had no idea that we would become such good friends. We both had little girls named Amber, and we did become friends and had so much fun together. We worked in an office full of ... well, let's just call them "interesting characters" and leave it at that.

One day Rebecca and I went to Kmart at lunchtime. She had a handicap parking permit, but this old white lady told her that she couldn't park there because there was nothing wrong with her, and could we just wait while she called the parking lot patrol? I thought the lady was joking and wanted to wait, but Rebecca said to the lady, "If you don't move I'll run you over." The lady took down her tag number and said the parking lot patrol would contact her with a court date. Rebecca was the equivalent to Tyler Perry's Madea; surely she would have backed into that woman.

At Christmastime one year we had an office luncheon, and when it was over Rebecca cleaned up all of the leftovers and told me to take what I wanted. Little did we know that two other people had dibs on the leftovers. I wanted to give them back, but Rebecca was like, "Oh well, they'll get over it."

Another time a coworker asked us about doing something romantic for her boyfriend. We gave her some tips, and on Monday we asked her how the weekend was. Poor fellow, had no clue. He wanted to know why she had candles and wine with soft music and finger foods. He told her, "We could have gone to Burger King and got a six-pack"!

Once when two new employees were hired, the manager assigned Rebecca to train the white girl and someone else to train the black girl. Within three hours Rebecca's trainee was ready to work on her own, but the other trainee had to train an extra two weeks and still had no clue what she was supposed to do. To keep her from looking bad, Rebecca gave her a job lead with another company.

Finally the day came for Rebecca to take her leave from ACC. It really wasn't goodbye, just time to move on to better things. When she handed in her resignation the manager put it in the trash. He didn't think she would leave. On the following Monday he received a call from the HR department letting him know that Rebecca had taken another job with ACC's top competitor. By then he knew his time was running out. ACC made her an offer to stay, but it was time for her to move on. ACC lost a lot of their business when she left. Rebecca eventually became the top black marketing rep in the southeast. After she made a name for herself she came to work at Legis, where I was working at the time. Bad and worst were together again! Legis was a walk in the park. Those were the fun days!

Chapter 12

The Brown Family: A Special Thanks

❧

A special thanks to the Brown family: Darren, Alma, Maria, Tia and Brandon. We laughed and shared a lot.

Another good memory of my time in Georgia is my relationship with my next-door neighbors Darren and Alma Brown. We all lived in the townhomes in Doraville and became very good friends. Thank God Alma was able to find me here in Maryland so we had the chance to reunite.

Neither of our families had a lot of money; we were all working people. So Alma and I used to help one another by sharing the groceries. If I had money I would take her shopping, and if she had money she would take me shopping. It was just awesome and so inspirational to be around both her and Darren. They have been together for over twenty-five years, and I could look to them for counsel when I wasn't sure if I was going to leave or stay with my now ex-husband.

One time Alma's church was having a youth dance group. They were short on kids, so they invited Tiff and Britt to perform along with them even though they were not members of the church. Every week Alma would pile all the kids—her daughters Maria and Tia, son Brandon, and my daughters Tiffanie and Brittney—into her van and take them all to the church. At this time I was not consistent with going to church (Alma is so proud of how involved I currently am with church), and neither of our husbands would dare step foot in the church. So Alma was the lone soldier who made sure the kids had a spiritual foundation. She made it fun, and my kids were excited about continuing to go with Alma and her kids to church.

The show was so beautiful. There was not a dry eye in that church. The dancers wore white tights, black leotards, and silver angel wings along with silver halos. Britt was the smallest out of the group. She was seven years old and had her front tooth missing. Tiff was ten at the time. First the group danced to Kirk Franklin's song "Lean on Me." My God, when the second song, Kirk Franklin's "You Are," came on—Wow, was it an awesome vision to experience! I still get chills remembering the performance. Just to listen to Kirk's lyrics and to see the kids pour their hearts out into the dance—even my ex-husband had tears in his eyes. Amber was enthralled too. She was four years old then, and we could never even take her to a movie theater because she made so much noise, but amazingly on this day the angels had her on her best behavior in the church.

We became even closer in 1999 when I had Jesurun. I could not keep those Brown kids out of my house. Maria used to love holding J and babysitting. She was wonderful, always doing big-girl things with all of the kids. And Brandon and Britt were regular partners in crime. Thank God for all of us those two turned out well.

It was just about a year ago that I reconnected with the Browns. Alma and Darren flew up from Georgia to purchase two cars from me. When Alma made the call she thought they were not going to be able to purchase even one car because prices were so high, but I searched for the lowest price and they were able to get two cars.

I remember how hard it was for our families to say goodbye when we left Georgia. Now Alma calls me her Oprah and I call her my Gayle.

Chapter 13

Hotel

⁂

Writing this book has brought back so many sad times in my life, like the time my kids and I spent living out of a hotel.

The kids and I had moved to Maryland to live with my dad after I left my husband. I got a job at a car dealership and worked on starting my life over with four kids to take care of on my own. We were all staying in my dad's single-family home when one day he suddenly yelled out and told me to come upstairs. Turns out he was angry because he thought my kids were trying to put voodoo on him. Yes, exactly. I was like, "What are you talking about?" and he said he found salt around his bed and he knew my kids did it. My first thought was that he was always eating in his bedroom; maybe he kicked the salt over or somehow spilled it himself. But of course his sidekick (my stepmother) jumped in and tried to explain, telling me the kids were in the room and they put salt around the bed. My dad said that we had to get out. He knew we had nowhere to go in Maryland, but he said he would not stay in the house with my kids that were trying to put voodoo on him, never mind the fact that none of us had any idea how to even do a voodoo curse.

Meanwhile, my kids were upstairs in their room and heard everything that was said. When I went back downstairs, they followed me, crying and saying, "Mommy, I swear it wasn't us. Mommy, that's not true!"

While I was reassuring the kids, my stepmother came into the room and tried to explain. "He is just mad. Let him calm down, because right now he's really mad and the salt being put around the bed is a serious thing." At that very moment I realized for the very first time that I was now old enough to say the reason I loved Sharon was because as a child growing up I hated my father Sylvester. Just think about it—she was just the lesser of two evils and went along with everything he did whether he was right or wrong; she didn't treat us any better than he did.

He was mad? I was hurt and angry that my father would put me and his four grandchildren out on the street because of a "salt curse." Later, when I explained to my mother about what had happened, her first response was that maybe his wife was trying to put voodoo on him. To this very day, we all still think she put the salt there and the kids got blamed for it.

But that didn't really matter at the time. I needed a place right away for me and the kids to live. The next day I found a vacancy at a Red Roof Inn—there was no time to even look for an apartment. The hotel was near my job at the dealership, which was good because sometimes I would get out very late. You know you can see a person at work every day and not know what is going on in their lives. I would be at work and would go in the bathroom to get on my knees and pray. I was realizing that maybe God was all I really had to rely on. I'd come to know that God had a plan for me and that he would work everything out for good, but I was ready for that good to start happening immediately. My children were on my mind constantly, but the worst thing was if I didn't go to work and make money we would not have had access to the hotel. We were truly just one step away from sleeping in the car. I would also have to drive the kids to their school near my dad's house, about a half hour away. I called my family and asked if someone would come down from New York to help us, just to babysit and be with the kids while I was at work. I was not comfortable going to work and leaving them alone in a hotel for hours. My young cousin Serena did come down to help for a couple of weeks, but then she was young and wanted to go home so she could run the streets with her boyfriend.

I felt smothered, like my world was crumbling down on me. My kids were being uprooted again, first from Georgia and now this. Would we ever be settled? This shuffling from place to place was a hard life, for the kids and for me. I tell you, it doesn't matter how much money you make, paying nearly $300 a week for a hotel and buying food every night becomes very costly. There was a grocery store directly across the street, but with no refrigerator, stove, or microwave I couldn't buy regular groceries to feed my kids. I was able to buy just the two-liter sodas that we could close and reuse, but I had to throw out a lot of food; as much as it hurt for me to waste it, I just couldn't store it. We lived on fast food from Taco Bell or McDonald's or had Domino's Pizza delivered to the room. There were plenty of nights that we would eat cold pizza that had stayed out from the night before. When I think back now, I see how God was watching over us and keeping us from food poisoning.

Besides not having basic kitchen appliances, we always knew the room wasn't really ours. This was a hotel, a place where most people were just passing through and where some went to cheat on their spouses. At night we could hear through the walls the people having sex in the next room. If my kids weren't asleep, they sure knew how to pretend they were. We even found a used condom under the bed in the first room they put us in, so I made them switch us to a different room. The second room was going to be as good as we could get. It was on the second floor and had two double beds. I tried to pretend that all five of us were just sharing one big bedroom. The cleaning lady was so nice she would give us extra towels, which we used as tablecloths or to stand on while taking a shower. We didn't use the hotel towels on our bodies because I'd bought us our own towels at Target. I even bought sheets, soap, comforter sets—everything to try to get the kids comfortable. I also bought them headphones so they could listen to music while they slept, instead of the sounds coming from the neighboring rooms.

At night, while the kids slept with their music on, I would just lie there and pray, wondering where we would be next week.

One day we got back to the room and the key didn't work. All of our things were inside. You could not get into the room until you paid for another week. Well, I had to put the kids in the car because it was so cold outside—it had to be in the thirties—while I went into the office to pay so that the manager could reactivate our key.

I have been through so much and I will always take the hand that God gives me, but it breaks my heart when my kids suffer with me. I knew I had to make a decision that was going to crush me. I told the kids I wanted them to go to New York with my cousin Serena and stay with my mother until I could get us somewhere to live. My precious, caring, loving children did not want to leave me. They said, "Ma, it's okay here. We have a bathroom, we have beds to share. It's okay, Mom, we are happy." All I could say was "God, I know you have a plan for my life, but all I ask for now is a place where my kids can be safe and that we can call home."

The lesson I took away from what I was going through was to treat everyone the same. I didn't have to be nasty to people. Instead, I could say "Good morning," "How are you doing?" "Have a nice day" or "Good evening." Those words that may seem simple to us can mean a lot to someone else. For some people, those few kind words may be the only pleasant moment in their lives that day. When I was at my low and feeling in the worst way, I knew that my help was going to come from the Lord. However, I still waited for someone to tell me it would be okay; I yearned for encouragement, and wished I could hear it from a person.

Eventually some temporary help came from an unexpected source. My stepsister called me and said we could come stay in her two-bedroom apartment. While I was appreciative for the offer, it didn't turn out to be a comfortable situation. I knew my stepsister was raised in a dysfunctional environment, so I should have expected craziness. She smoked inside, so the house would smell horrible from the lingering odor of stale cigarettes. She also never had food. I would go to the store every other week and spend about $300 or $400 on groceries. She did the same thing that my dad did when we lived with him: ate up all the food. She didn't have much furniture, so in exchange for letting me stay there I let her use one of my TVs and I paid half her rent.

I was very grateful until one day two of her friends went out with me to the BET soundstage in Maryland. Well, they mentioned to me that my stepsister would tell them she couldn't wait until I got out; she said I didn't do anything or help her. God is good though. I didn't even have to explain myself; instead, I let her mouth do all the talking. One day I hadn't gone to the bank and she ran her mouth in front of her friends, telling them that I better hurry up and give her some money. Her friends' reaction was "I thought you said Tinge didn't give you anything." God exposed her. I have never mentioned this to her, but it hurt me so much. While I was at her house she had stuff she never had; she had lots of food and extra money, and I cooked. I never mentioned it because I knew it was God that used her for me and the kids to have a place to stay, but now you know.

The other hurtful part was she told me that my dad had said she shouldn't take us in. (Do you hear this? He not only kicked us out, he also tried to make sure that no one else took us in.) But she said to me that she told him, "It's my apartment; I will do what I want to do." I really cannot say I believed her as much as I wanted to because I have witnessed on other occasions how afraid they were to stand up to my father. What my stepsister didn't know was God used her to get us out of the Red Roof Inn. What I didn't know was that she would constantly go over to my dad's house and talk about me, going along with everything he and my stepmother would say, and then turn around and speak badly about me to her friends. I cannot say I was surprised by it, but I did forgive her; my dad can be very manipulative.

My Lord.

Chapter 14

In Memory of Uncle Butch:
From Drug Addict to Wanting to Live
Joseph Nathan Singleton
September 10, 1954 – March 22, 2004

⁓

Yet if they **Repent** *in the land to which they have been carried captive,*
and turn and pray there, saying, We have sinned, we have done wrong, and have
dealt wickedly.
2 Chronicles 6:37

You know they say a parent shouldn't show favorites between her children, but they must have made that rule up and not told Grandma about it, because clear as day my uncle Butch the methadone addict was her favorite. Yes, I said methadone addict. He started out as a heroin addict but then tried to come off the heroin and got stuck with methadone. My grandmother always covered for him and would fight or argue with anyone that confronted him. He knew that and he gloated on it; he would start the argument and sit back and watch my grandmother finish it.

Butch was especially good for stealing and wearing other people's clothes. What he would do is hide the clothes in the backyard of the building or the basement. No matter how high he was, he knew he had to change clothes before he walked up to that fourth floor. When he got caught stealing clothes he would sit there and watch my grandma argue for him.

Once again we were some bad kids. We didn't know that the methadone was medicine for Uncle Butch; all we knew was when he drank that stuff his voice would change and his facial expression would drop. The worst part of it all was when my grandfather was asleep I remember a couple of times watching them—my uncle and my grandmother—steal my granddad's money. We had a junkie in the house, so Pops used to sleep with his money in his pocket, and one day he caught his son with his hand in his pocket. Pops had these huge hands, and he grabbed my uncle. When my grandmother tried to stop it he grabbed her too. Guess what? She was the lookout. No one could pry his hands off of my grandma's and uncle's necks. They did everything until he finally decided on his own to let them go. That was the last time they ever went into Pops' pockets.

This was the same uncle that never had any children. He lived with my grandmother until he died when he was in his late forties. We never saw him with any girlfriend. Grandma would give him money to keep him from being killed; she thought he would try to rob someone and they would kill him. She had no idea that she never helped him by doing that.

My uncle never slept in a bed. In fact, he slept sitting up in a chair in the living room. We were scared to let the covers touch the floor because we kids thought the mice would climb on them and get in the bed with us, yet we would see them playing around his feet all the time. Because we didn't know any better, we all thought that if he would ever lie down to sleep he would die, just never wake up again. We used to think he was the Elephant Man. I also remember how he would nod out when he was walking in the streets. He would go all the way to where his knees were bent but would never hit the ground. We thought he would die if he hit the ground. The worst thing is everyone knew one another so no one would bother him in the streets and somehow, high as a kite and feeling good as could be, he would always manage to make it home, nodding out for maybe ten or twenty blocks. Shoot, I guess that was his hard day's work just making it home every day. Luckily for him, he only got robbed maybe two or three times by people that didn't know my family.

The funniest thing is that as a grown-up you are embarrassed, but children love all people. My oldest daughter, Tiff, was good for running up to Uncle Butch, giving him a hug, and trying to talk to him. She loved her uncle Bitch—yes, that's right, Uncle Bitch! For some reason she just could not say "Butch." While he was up there slurring his words, scratching, and nodding, of course she didn't know better, being no more than three or four years old. Sometimes his friends from the methadone clinic would walk with him and

Tiff, as happy as she was, one day said, "Hi, Uncle Bitch." His friend was so surprised and laughed so hard!

I am sorry to say that I do not remember him ever being happy. When I was younger there wasn't much of anything I could do but watch him self-destruct. I didn't understand why he was on drugs and why for so long. I thought drugs were usually a phase that some people went through.

All through my childhood I saw the effects drugs had on people's lives. I know that when all you have known is drugs, it's not easy to get away from it. Frequently on the television you'll see a black man getting arrested for drugs or guns and the first thing said is "He is a product of his environment." I will not say that isn't true, but I have to say that not everyone who grows up in that environment becomes a product of it. It would have been so easy for me to make that excuse for myself, to say, "This is where I'm from so this must be what I am," but I never did that. I saw firsthand how drugs ruined lives, and I wanted more for myself—and for my kids too. So now I say thank you, God, for not letting me be a product of my environment.

My uncle Butch started doing drugs at the young age of fifteen. Not any ordinary drugs either—he was on heroin. Uncle Butch essentially died at that very young age; for years afterward he was a walking dead man. His shell wandered the world until he turned fifty-one years old; then he was diagnosed with terminal cancer and was told by doctors he had six months to live. He never had children, and to my knowledge he never even had a girlfriend. When he died there would be no one to carry on the legacy; it would stop at him. How awful and sad.

My uncle Butch never cared about dying. We would always try to get him off the drugs, but he didn't care that they were killing him. He would go out into the streets every day, rain or shine. In fact, you would mistake him for a man with a nine-to-five job. He would go out fresh, straight, and alert, but he never came back the same way. Coming back he would be doing his junkie nod all the way home. But like I mentioned before, no matter how high out of his mind he was, Uncle Butch always made it back home.

When you are a kid you say things having no idea what the meaning or effect of it may be. I have to say we were so ashamed of Uncle Butch that we would often turn in the other direction. We would say we wished he would leave and not come back. We said we wished he would be put out of his misery. He didn't care about life, so why should we care about him? As an adult I know how malicious those comments were. In fact, Uncle Butch didn't want to live because he couldn't stop inflicting pain on himself or his family.

An old friend of the family came to the door and said that Uncle Butch had been hit by a bus and taken to the hospital. We were very scared because no matter how bad off he was he was still blood family. My mother and my aunts Ann, Sheila, and Valerie went to the hospital along with my uncle Anthony to see his condition. We thought he would be hanging on by a thread. Surely he would be hard to look at after being hit by a bus. But although Uncle Butch had a death wish that he pursued by injecting that plague into his body, God showed mercy on him over and over. When my mother and aunts arrived at Harlem Hospital, in fear of the way he may look and his condition, they sent my uncle to go into the room alone to see him first. Uncle Butch was high as usual and with hardly a scratch on him, so my uncle went back out to the emergency room to get the sisters. They walked into the room and he was sitting up, and when they asked him what happened it turned out the bus didn't hit him, he was nodding and walked into the bus. He had come out of the subway station on 161st and Amsterdam Avenue and was making his way just one block over to 160th Street. When he went to cross the street the bus was driving past and he misjudged it. In his mind the bus had already passed, but in reality it was coming upon him. He stepped down and walked into the bus. The impact left him with only minor bumps and bruises. God gave Uncle Butch more time in this world to turn his life around.

Everyone was relocated with family when my grandmother's apartment building burned completely down. Because of the way he lived his life, no one wanted Uncle Butch or trusted him enough to take him in. So he went and rented a room from this older lady. My grandmother would give him money weekly to pay his rent. He would go to my aunt Valerie's house every day and sit and watch television with my grandma in her room. My aunt would feed him and let him stay until it was time for them to go to bed. Well, it turned out that Uncle Butch was taking the money for his methadone and was sleeping on the subway every night. He would get on the train and ride it from end to end. We found that out from a friend who was riding the train late one night and mentioned that they saw him. Afterwards he was confronted by my family, and they decided the money wouldn't be given to him but directly to where he was staying. There were very dangerous people that would attack the homeless in New York, and we had no clue that was going on with him.

Uncle Butch tried another route of getting money. My grandmother of course supported him his entire life; he never worked a job. She still gave him money to use for traveling back and forth to the room he was renting. One day my family received another phone call from the police station. Apparently Uncle Butch had been arrested for jumping the turnstile—and in New York that meant literally jumping over the subway turnstile—to avoid paying his fare. Again he'd taken the money he had received from my grandmother and used it for his methadone. Needless to say, they had to bail him out. The police would not immediately arrest you for jumping the turnstile, but if you did it often enough you would be arrested.

Uncle Butch got very sick and was in and out of the hospital. Even though we were all mad at him, he was still family and we were going to visit and see how he was doing. The last hospital visit didn't turn out well. He was diagnosed with terminal cancer. They kept him in Columbia Presbyterian, and I watched my aunts and mother go visit him every day. You see, he was not going to be alone. The hospital kept him for a while, and then he was transferred to a place where terminally ill patients could just be kept comfortable for whatever time they had left on this Earth. This place was over an hour away, and it cost seventy-five dollars to take a taxi there. This was in 2003, when I was making very decent money. I bought a used Maxima and sent the car to New York so that my family could use it to visit Uncle Butch.

There were a couple of nuns that would pray with Uncle Butch every day. In his final months he looked his very best. You see, after poisoning his body for nearly thirty-seven years he found out how life could be worth living. Uncle Butch went cold turkey and with all the clarity he now had, he told my aunt Ann that he didn't want to die. I was in Maryland, so I didn't have to experience watching his deterioration over the months. He was praying and going to Bible study with the nuns. I am so grateful that Uncle Butch had the chance to repent and ask for God's forgiveness before he died. He was in so much pain, and the only thing he could have for it was Oxycontin; if he wasn't asleep he was in pain. The last time my family visited, his stomach had hardened and they knew it wouldn't be long.

He did not want to die, he said. He had his brother Tony who would sit with him and talk for hours until visiting was over. He had his sisters by his side. That was something he'd never given either one of them the chance to do because he was always high and unapproachable.

I had planned a trip because I knew this time was so hard on my family. My uncle Tony didn't want to go; he was superstitious and said if the plane crashed there needed to be someone left to carry on the family. I loved Vegas, so I paid for a suite at the Venetian Hotel, purchased four plane tickets, and told my mother, my aunt Ann, and cousin Sheka to come and get away for a little rest for an early Mother's Day. These were three good mothers, and I wanted them to go relax.

My uncle Butch died that following week. Aunt Ann took it hard. She thought he let go and gave up because no one had gone to visit him. Skeeter, my twin brothers' uncle, told her it was nonsense to think that way. Maybe while they were visiting he was not letting go because he didn't want to leave them even though he was in enormous pain. Many times he didn't even know when they were visiting because of all the morphine they had to put him under. Now he was resting and not tired anymore, and he knew we all loved him.

When Uncle Butch died, he found God. He died knowing he was loved and he was not alone, but that family would always come together through the hard times. He was cremated, and his urn is kept at my aunt Valerie's house.

Chapter 15

Discernment

⚊⁓

And my God shall supply all your need according to His riches in glory by Christ Jesus.
Philippians 4:19

Be ye not unequally yoked together.
2nd Corinthians 6:14

I am a female who has always been surrounded by men. Let's face it, the car business is a good ole boy network, a man's world. I succeeded in the business, rising from entry-level worker to finance manager, general manager, and soon to be the owner of my own dealership. I am proud of the fact that I didn't have to sleep with any bosses to get to where I am. I worked very hard and was very proud of all the knowledge God gave me on what I was doing. Listen, ladies, it feels so good to be able to speak toe to toe with the men and actually know what I'm speaking about and be right at it. I am a woman and I like men, so yes, I have slept with men (obviously—I do have four children). However, you don't have to do that for a job; hard work is the only thing that will really get you to where you want to be.

Also, ladies, I am a single mother and I can tell you that what we have to understand as single parents is our kids' well-being comes first. I have come to the conclusion that I am a mother first and single second. I want to say that again: We are mothers first and single second. I have always been very mindful of who I bring around my children; in this world there are pedophiles and a lot of mess out there. I'm scared because the pedophiles prey on single parents in order to get close to the children, and I cannot risk my children's well-being just because I need companionship. I am so scared of all the crimes going on against kids and how Satan is attacking our kids. Our children are depending on us to keep their innocence, keep them safe, and no man is more important to me than my children. Sure I miss companionship, but thank God I have God and the children so I'm never lonely.

I haven't dated in about four years now, but when I do date I don't bring just any man around my children; you don't want your kids to have the memory of seeing their mom with different men. I don't want to be alone, but when the time is right—on God's time, I know, not mine—he will send me my husband. I do pray that God will give me a nudge if it looks like I am going to miss my special man, though.

I pray to God almost every night to send me a good man, a good supportive husband so that we could have some money and be happy. I know money doesn't mean everything, and I know they say it can't buy you love. Well, being broke can mess up love. So I'd rather be a married, successful, happy couple. I pray these words to God: "Lord, you have directed the paths of my life, and I know you tried to warn me and open up my eyes, but being hardheaded I didn't see it. So, Father, I know my choices of men have not been pleasing, but please, Lord, I'm not picking anymore. All I ask is that you send me my husband and if I miss him in front of me send down a sign. God, I'm going to wait on you to send me not what I think is the man for me but who you think is the right man for me."

It's been so long since I've dated that my two older daughters—Tiff, twenty-one years old, and Britt, eighteen years old—are saying, "Mom, you need to go out and get a boyfriend because it's only going to be you, J, and Amber and we have to screen these guys before we leave home." I told them I have to get all these kids out the house and then focus on me. Right now it's not about me, and I have decided not to try to pick another man because my choices have all been bad. I want to tell you some stories about the men in my life. Ladies, I'm telling you these things because I want you to trust your feelings and your gift of discernment so that you don't travel down the same paths I have.

After my divorce was in process I was actually considering getting married again. This was really before I rededicated my life back to Jesus. I was dating this guy named Eddie for about two years and we became engaged. He was a very clean-cut, very sharp-dressing individual, and we worked at the same dealership. I was already employed there when he got a job there. I know you shouldn't date people you work with, but when you're working twelve-hour days every Saturday you don't have much time to go out and meet people. Well anyway, I thought this was my Prince Charming. Finally, here was somebody on the same level as I was. He was a manager, and when we went to dinner he paid cash but had a gold credit card in his pocket. We would hook up after work. (At this time my children were in New York. Because of the hours I worked, the kids would go up and stay with my family during the summer so they wouldn't be home alone doing nothing. Of course, that meant I was home alone during my off hours.)

I was making really good money at this time, about an average of $15,000 to $17,000 a month—yes, that's correct, and a far cry from when I started out making $21,000 a year. I was so worried that someday I would go to the bank and find out my direct deposit did not go through, but thank God that never happened. This man was a manager, so I thought he was making some money too. He was around six foot two and 170 pounds. He always dressed to impress, looked like he was well off financially.

We dated for two years or so and of course still lived at separate addresses. The one thing I was not going to do was have a man living with me before we were married. Sorry to say that bit of morality was because of my children, not because I was living right. Like I said earlier, I had not rededicated myself at this point. I didn't have to be a rocket scientist to cover my children. I am like a lioness protecting her cubs when it comes to them; my guard is always up no matter who the person is. I would rarely leave my kids unsupervised with anyone. So we were dating and having sex but not living together.

This man had an ex-wife with kids. I met his entire family, and they were very nice people. In fact, the first time I went to his sister's house for Thanksgiving she and his mom made it a point to tell me that he only dated white women and they were very shocked when they saw that I was black. I laughed because I didn't care about that; I'm secure in my life. They could have told me something important, like the fact that he was a very moody person.

One day I was at Eddie's house and brother man went into the room and was walking back and forth. I was like, "What's up with you?" He smoked cigarettes and of course I didn't, but as long as he went outside I didn't care. He would go outside if he was in my house but not if he was in his apartment. So I told him to open the patio door. I didn't care; it was late, and we'd worked a long day. I was lying on his sofa and said, "It's your house—go ahead." Well, folks, he proceeded to pull out this pipe. I come from New York, so when you hear anything about a pipe immediately you think crack. I said, "What the Hell! You are a freaking crackhead!" I got up and was getting my stuff on and getting out of there. I'm like, "What the *BLEEP*! You are a *BLEEPING* crackhead. Are you crazy?" I started to get pissed because this brother man was sitting there laughing his butt off at my reaction. He had to grab me just to try to get me to listen to him tell me it was not a crack pipe. Well, you sophisticated DC/MD people smoke weed/marijuana out of a pipe, but in New York I'm used to seeing them use cigar paper or the white cigarette paper. I couldn't believe this grown-behind man in his forties was still smoking pot. I thought that was a young kids' thing. I told him to get uncomfortable with me again. Because he had gotten comfortable enough to think he could sit around me and smoke weed.

That definitely explained the moodiness and the way his face would look so droopy at times and his lips, oh my goodness, were so black. Well, me and my stupid self tried to give him the benefit of the doubt. I listened to his reasoning, and just like any junkie they will always have excuses. He said, "You don't see people selling their houses and losing stuff over weed." Duh! Silly me said, "You're right. Just don't smoke that stuff around me." I continued to hang out with him. I grew up around people doing drugs, which made me have absolutely no urge to do it. I saw what the cocaine and crack was doing to some of my family and friends in New York. In fact, my older kids' dad was a pothead. Like I said, that pipe thing just threw me for a loop.

Over the next year or so I learned a lot more about him. One night we had gone to his friend's home in Annapolis to watch the fight (no, I'm not the typical woman—I love boxing and football. I am Floyd Mayweather's number one fan.) Not my crowd of people, but it was a beautiful home in a very exclusive subdivision. As we were leaving his friend's huge house, this man tells me that his ex-wife was living in their house which was even bigger than this one. I said, "Wow!" I'm thinking Eddie must be loaded if he is paying the mortgage on that house and rent at his apartment. In a moment I went from being so secure to saying to myself, "Wow, my house must be really little." I was living in my dad's home, which had an in-ground pool that we really only used on Fourth of July cookouts. It also had this really nice-size backyard. But suddenly I felt like his kids must really think my house was little.

I started noticing some things after that. Like every time I would see the kids they would always have on the same clothes. Well, I thought maybe that was a ploy, like they wore one set of clothes with me and another set of clothes when they visited their dad. I also noticed they enjoyed the pool more than my kids and when it was time to go home they didn't want to leave. On Father's Day I got tickets to take all the kids to the Universal Soul Circus. Afterwards we were going to pass their house on the way to mine, but he decided to take me home first and then take the kids back home. I assumed he wanted to spend a little of Father's Day with just them on the ride home.

Then one day we were going down to his family reunion in Virginia. It was near the end of summer, so my kids were still in New York with my family. He had to go pick up his boys and asked me to just meet him at his mom's house. While I was there we got on the subject of how beautiful her townhome was and how he told me about the huge house that his ex and the boys lived in. His nice honest mother was like, "Girl, what house are you talking about? They live right up the street in an apartment and I don't see them, only when he brings them over." I told his mother that he told me they lived in this huge house and he even pointed out a house. I asked her if they'd lost the house and she said, "Girl, no. They never had a big house. What they lost was a rented townhome they lived in." Wow, another sign from God and I didn't listen.

I was house shopping at this time. I'd been renting my father's house. Yes, I was now renting from the same man who had once put us out on the street. The arrangement was another attempt at reconciliation that never worked out. It started when my dad's father, Mr. Craft, was moving out of his home and into a place with his girlfriend, and my dad was going to be moving into Mr. Craft's house. That would leave my father with two mortgages to pay. At the time my brother had his own place and my stepsister was not in a position to afford the monthly payment. I'm certain I was the last choice, but he ended up renting the house to me. Originally he'd said the house would be mine and the kids', but that never came to pass. My dad did not want to sell me his house and I didn't want to keep paying his mortgage and fixing up his place. And so it was time to look for a place that my kids and I could truly call our own.

I had my loan set up already approved for a $900,000 home on my qualifications alone. I had no intention of using anywhere near that much though. Eddie decided to go out with me and look. Every model home we went into it became "baby this" and "baby that," as in "Baby, we need a basement so when the boys come visit they can feel like they are home." Then it was "let's do this," "let's get that." It turned out to be house shopping for us.

The home I decided on optioned out at $850,000. I said, "There's no way I can do that by myself." I heard, "Baby, we can do it together. We get married, move in, and we will be fine." Well, I started to like the idea of getting married. I could have a husband to come home to and cuddle with every day. I got away from the original plan; now it was all about my feelings. I agreed we should get the house together, so the next morning I called the loan officer and told him I was going to have Eddie go on my loan. Brother man then gave the loan officer all of his information.

Well, the next day the loan officer said, "Shanise, I am going to tell you what I would tell my own daughter. Do not buy a house with this man. How long have you known him?" I said I'd known him about three years and we were talking about getting married. He said, "Before you do that, get to know about this man. And do not buy anything with him."

That was pretty strong information coming from an outsider. I marched right over to this man and said, "You better tell me the truth right now. I'm sick of all the lies and I am breaking it off right now." He said he was sorry. Turns out he never had a house; in fact, that townhouse I told you about earlier was not on his credit report. He didn't have a personal car because he could not qualify for one. I was so mad. He'd told me one lie after another until I didn't know what to believe. I told him I wanted to see his credit report, and when he showed it to me I couldn't figure out why in the heck he would even embarrass himself by giving the loan officer his information. This man never paid one single person anything. Oh, and remember when I said he had a GOLD card in his wallet?

I questioned him about it, and he said he used it as a form of ID. Wow, the card did not even work.

I was so angry I called my aunt and told her about it. And you know what she told me? "He was trying to impress you. He sees everything you have going on and is just trying to build himself up. You're going to get that a lot being a young successful woman." She said to give him a chance, talk to him. I didn't pay attention to the sign from God and told my aunt okay.

By this time I knew his credit was bad and he could not go on the loan with me, so I decided I would get a house payment I could handle by myself. I warned him he could not keep any secrets and that if we were going to do this I needed to take care of the bills myself. Since at that time I could handle bills better, we decided to set up an account together and I would pay for both houses from there. Well, that didn't work for long because I had to take a step back and say, "You have more going out than coming in. That's my money you are spending." So that account got closed very quickly.

Motorcycle season was coming up, and he was always talking about wanting a motorcycle. This man was in his forties and always wanted to get his own motorcycle. We ended up getting the motorcycle ... or I should say *I* ended up getting the motorcycle. I had called the bank to check on the rates to finance one. I figured it would be about $150 a month. I agreed to get the loan for him; however, I paid cash for the motorcycle and just had him pay me the monthly payments straight into my bank account. The craziest thing was that I went to the store and paid for the motorcycle and then he went with his friend to pick it up. I later found out that his friend had to drive the motorcycle home and take him to a park to teach this clown how to ride it. He could have killed himself—I had no idea he didn't know how to ride a motorcycle. After a couple of months the motorcycle ended up being stolen from in front of his apartment. The insurance company went to pay the loan off and then said that there wasn't a lien on it. This bamma thought he hit the jackpot and said since there is no lien we could just keep making the payments on the bike and use the money to buy a couple of things. I told him, "Oh no, we're not," and I took the money and put it back in my account.

A few months went by and he seemed to be getting a little more responsible. We started to look for a house to rent until my house was ready, which was going to be a year-long process. I had found a place, and we decided to let him move in with us. By this time my kids knew him very well. If I was going to be in a long-term relationship I figured we could combine our two rent payments into one and move in together. Well, guess what I found out? To sum it up, the grown man that I was in love with that did not own a car, that had very bad credit, that didn't have enough money to cover anything I wanted to do without letting his lights get turned off— oh yeah, I forgot I had to loan him money when his lights were disconnected—this brother man let me write the letter to his apartment leasing office to say he would not be renewing, then they called me back to tell me they didn't have a tenant by that name. Turns out the name listed on the lease was his BROTHER. God gave me another sign, but I just made an excuse for him. I figured, Okay, when he got divorced his brother had to help him get an apartment.

It was 2004 and the BMW 645 was being introduced to the states. I was one of the first people to get one. This was an $80,000 car that I custom ordered and had to wait six months for them to build. This was my very first large purchase of a car, and it was very exciting. I had a logon name and password that I could use to go onto the website and monitor every bolt and piece they put on the car. During this time I also purchased my daughter Tiff a brand-new Pontiac for her sixteenth birthday. It was funny because at the time Eddie was working for Pontiac and was acting like a big shot that *we* were buying my daughter a car, trying to help me pick out the colors and all. I didn't know he had told everyone that until I got down to the dealership and one of my friends told me. In fact, this brother man went so far as to flash my platinum credit cards and say that he was the card holder and he wouldn't put anything less than platinum in his wallet. Since our coworkers really didn't care for him, they happily told me what he did—yeah, that's another story. (God takes care of babies and fools, remember. He took care of me on that one. Brother man didn't make any purchases on there that could have jammed me up, and I closed the card out and got an entirely different account number.)

Anyway, the time came when my car was finally ready. I got the phone call from the dealership, and by the time I got there everyone was all over the car. I was the first person to get a 645 in through that dealership. There was a waiting list for over a year, and I talked myself right into getting one the same day I went.

Well, Eddie went with me to the dealership.... Listen, people, I know how you feel when you are trying to buy something and your spouse is acting like a complete ass. So many times I would see couples arguing and acting stupid and nasty towards one another in the dealership. Well, I was talking to the salesman, who by the way ended up later getting a lot of referrals from me—he was great. My fiancé decided he wanted me to get specialized tags with *his* nickname on them. Yes, my head swung around so fast I got whiplash. I told him, "You must be joking. I'm not doing that." He then proceeded to tell me since I bought Tiff a car he thought he was going to get the next car. I asked him, "What made you think that? Tiff is my daughter, and what I do for my kids has nothing to do with you." By this time the poor sales guy is sitting there just taking it all in.

Brother man next took it upon himself to tell the guy WE are not buying the car, WE changed our mind. Then he told me that with the house and all he didn't think it was a good idea. I told the salesperson, "Yes, I am buying this car. Call me when it's ready to be picked up" (it still had to go through the inspection process). Brother man got up and said, "If you take this car out of here then it's over between us," to which I said, "Okay, GOODBYE." The salesman laughed, and brother man was so mad he stormed out of the dealership. David, my salesman, told me, "Good for you, Shanise. That guy is a jerk. He's rude; you don't want to be with him anyway. You are too good. You are too nice for him."

I tried to stick my chest out and hold my head up, but I was so embarrassed. Mind you, I would be embarrassed for the customers that did this sort of thing in my dealership—I couldn't believe it was happening to me. I did get my car and never let brother man drive it. I kept it for two years before selling it.

Well, of course he came back to me and pleaded for us to get back together. I agreed and we ended up getting engaged. The funny part is that he wanted to surprise me, so he asked my mom to come down from New York and he told her first. He pulled her aside and told her we were going out to dinner and he was going to ask me to marry him. I knew it was going to happen eventually, but not at that time. My mom immediately ruined the surprise by telling me (it was her way of warning me), "He's going to ask you to marry him. Are you sure you want to do this? I think you need to think about this one before you do it." It wasn't a very long engagement, so I won't waste much time talking about it. We did get engaged, and he thought he had full control over me. The ring was gorgeous. It was a round diamond ring with three stones totaling three and a half carats—two and a half carats in the middle and a half carat on each end.

The final straw came when I decided to go on a family trip to Disney World. I took a total of thirteen people, kids and adults. I left from Maryland with my children and his two boys (mind you, one was not his biological child, but I didn't want to leave the kid out), and my mother, aunts, and cousins left from New York. We were going to meet up at the airport in Florida. Everyone was excited to go, but to this day I think this kid's mother coached him to act up and run me off. This little boy whined the entire time we were on the plane. None of the other kids would sit with him, so I had to make him sit next to me. The flight down was very nice. Everyone was having fun playing games and watching movies.

When we landed we were walking through the airport; in Florida you have to get on the train to get to the baggage claim. Well, I had to hold this little boy's hand, and it felt just like I was pulling a ton of bricks. I kept telling him to come on, hurry up, and we kept having to wait for him. It never dawned on me to check his shoes. This little kid had on a pair of tennis shoes two sizes too big. I was so upset. I couldn't imagine sending my kid all the way to Florida like that knowing that he would be doing a lot of walking. I got on the phone and cussed my fiancé out. I told him it made absolutely no sense that this kid had on shoes big enough to fit his brother. Do you know the fool had the nerve to tell me that the little boy threw a tantrum in the store over those shoes, so his foolish mother bought them just to shut him up?

We tried everything to keep those shoes on this kid's feet. We put two safety pins in, but that didn't work because the bad ass kept messing with the pins and scratched himself so we had to take them out. I couldn't let him go on any of the rides because I was scared his shoes would fall off while on the ride. He kept whining the entire time. I felt so bad for his brother because he annoyed him so bad and he couldn't have fun with the other kids. I contemplated buying him shoes but could not bring myself to do it. I already paid for the trip. I told his mother to just send the kids with spending money, so tell me why did they only have $50 in their pocket when we would be in Florida for an entire week? And that's not even the worst part.

Just to sum up the ending of the trip, the little boy had asthma and his mother did not bother to put his pump in his bag. He had such a severe attack that it very nearly ended in a bad way. He was in the bedroom with all the kids, and my cousin came out and said that this boy's breathing was very hard. I told the brother to call his mother because I was going to take him to the hospital and I needed all of his insurance information. The mother told me he would be okay and that I didn't need to bother. I asked her why she didn't send all his medications with him, and her response was that he had been well so she didn't think he would need his medication. I explained to her exactly how deep the breaths were, that I could see his ribs.

By this time I decided we had to go. The family I rented the house from left all the emergency numbers there, so I called the hospital and they gave me directions. My cousin went with me to the hospital. By the time we got him there the boy's lips were blue. He had no oxygen coming in. They immediately rushed him to the back and started him on the nebulizer. They tried that about three times and it wasn't helping. Finally they put him on oxygen and transported him by ambulance to the children's hospital. Of course we had no clue about Florida, and since only one person could go in the ambulance neither of us went. My cousin and I rode together to find the hospital. I tried to call his mother but couldn't reach her because she had gone out with her boyfriend. Eventually I got a hold of my fiancé and whaled into him that I would have to get stuck with something like this.

Once the boy finally got stable, I went back to the house just to change clothes and then headed back to the hospital. This was when the other kids told me that he kept holding his breath trying to stop breathing. You know kids will tell the truth. Apparently when we were all getting into the rented passenger van, one of my cousins sat next to this boy and he wasn't breathing. They kept calling him and calling him, and when she was about to run and get us he got up and started laughing and said, "I got you. I can act like

I'm dead." I was so furious. I believed this kid was Satan's spawn. When I got back to the hospital I asked him if he was holding his breath again to make himself sick, and this little problem child said YES.

We were scheduled to go home the next day. I got on the phone and told my fiancé that one of them better get on the next flight to Florida because I was going home. If I hadn't experienced it myself no one would have ever convinced me that a child could be so ruthless and bad. His mother finally caught a flight down. I asked the older brother if he wanted to go to the hospital to see his mother, and he said NO, he wanted to stay with me and my family. He wouldn't even speak to her on the telephone. He told me the little brother always ruined everything. By this time I was guessing that he terrorized the big one and got away with it all the time. So I ended up letting the older brother fly back to Maryland with us to take him to his dad until his mother got back. Guess what? He didn't even want to go with his dad, my fiancé; he wanted to stay with me. At this point I said, "Something is wrong here."

A long time ago I heard Bill Cosby do a standup comedy show in which he spoke about this woman on an airplane with a crying baby. The kid cried and threw a tantrum the entire flight. Well, the mother wouldn't give in to him, and the flight attendants and the passengers were all angry with the mother. When the flight landed the father, who was waiting at the gate, asked, "Honey, how was your flight?" The mother stood there out of breath, with her hair all out of place, then that woman pulled her hand back, balled up her fist, punched him in the face and said, "Take your kid!"

I didn't punch brother man, but at the same moment I thought about what getting married to him would mean: I would be the stepmother to these kids. That's when I said, "No way, José." That was the straw that broke the camel's back. I had a beautiful three-and-a-half-carat engagement ring that I had just gotten insured for over $20k, but I took the ring off my finger and gave it back. It was not worth it. I told him I would not be good for him because I could not accept his kids. My kids are no angels, but I always taught them that no one likes a fresh, disrespectful, unruly child. I could not teach my kids one set of values and let his come around and be completely different. Also I would never let them continuously ruin things for my children.

People asked why I gave the ring back. Honestly, I didn't know how he all of a sudden came into the money to buy it. Some of our mutual friends thought he set up my car being stolen because he had driven it to his house and all of a sudden he called me to ask me if I came over to take the car because it wasn't outside. I even had the police officer who came to the scene to take the report ask me if I thought he had anything to do with my Corvette convertible getting stolen. (At the time I said, "Of course not; he had nothing to gain.") Many of my friends speculated he had something to do with my car being stolen; however, I never found anything to prove it. I just gave back the ring. If it was his savings, I didn't want to take it. I told him to sell it back to the store; I was not marrying him. I broke up with him instantly and never looked back.

He bashed me for a while, telling all of our friends he didn't know why I did that to him. He even lied and told one guy that I took his season football tickets. He couldn't afford tickets. In fact, I had to show him for the liar he was and say the contract and tickets were mine and I just was going to let him go to the games with me. I heard for almost a year that he kept saying it should not have gone down like that and I shouldn't have broken up with him. Oh well. I finally did it. This man was no good for me from the start. I can tolerate a lot and give the benefit of the doubt to everyone, but when my kids voiced their concerns I felt completely differently. After I finally broke up with him I later found out my kids didn't like him; they only put up with him because they thought he made me happy. Apparently he asked my daughter Britt to get him some water and she did a Craig on *Fridays* when he picked up the dirty ice and put it in his dad's drink. Let's just say my nice little daughter watches a lot of television, and therefore she didn't go above and beyond to make sure the glass was exactly clean.

I made it clear to my kids that it is not about just my happiness, we all have to be happy, and they should never again keep their concerns or feelings bottled up. They are smart enough to voice their opinions. I taught them how to respect their elders and be responsible children, so they are allowed to speak within reason and without being out of line. I cannot stress this enough to single parents. I can say it over and over like a broken record. No one should be placed before your children, and definitely not between the relationship you've built up.

Chapter 16

Mice and Me

⌒

I know they say mice are more afraid of you than you are of them. Well, not in my case or my kids'. I remember four bad experiences with mice.

After Tiff was born I was sitting on the bed in my mother's apartment speaking with her father Anthony. We had mouse traps throughout the house trying to catch this mouse. New York had a huge rat problem. I guess I have to thank God my encounters were with the babies, the mice. Well, as we were sitting there talking Anthony said, "Shorty," which of course is what he called me, "Shorty, don't get scared. Pass me the mouse trap." I said, "What are you talking about?" and he laughed and looked down. Oh my goodness! I took off running to the door. As we were talking a mouse had walked right past Anthony's foot and he'd stepped on the tail so it was stuck under his foot. He got it out of the house, but of course without help from me; my cousin had picked up the glue trap and given it to him.

Another encounter happened one day when we were getting ready to go out to Atlantic City, New Jersey. I always had a habit of shaking my shoes out before I put them on. I didn't even understand why I did it, because if anything ever dropped out I would have been scared stiff. Well, that day I was in a rush to finish getting dressed and I put my boot on without shaking it out first. Immediately my toe felt something moving inside. I took that boot off and shook it out and OMG, it was a mouse! I threw the boot all the way from one room to another. I had a tough time wearing boots for a while after that.

I didn't know there were different types of mice in New York. I guess I had the city mice up there, because down here in Maryland they call them field mice. That must be what grass gets you, field mice.

Well, we all like to get the glue traps to catch the mice, but what I never took into consideration was who would dispose of that mouse when I caught it. One day when we lived in my dad's house Britt had company over to spend the night. We knew a field mouse had gotten into the house through the dryer vent in the laundry room. Just my luck, the mouse decided to get caught. It got stuck on the glue strip and we, me and the kids, were all scared to get it. I had Tiffanie call her friend, but of course it would have taken time for him to get there and we could hear the mouse trying to get off the trap. Yes, we could hear it, but we couldn't see it because we were all scared to look into the kitchen.

Britt's friend who was spending the night said, "I will pick it up. I'm not scared; we have them in our house." So I padded her up, made her put on the kitchen mittens, put plastic bags over the mittens, and gave her a trash bag, the broom, and the dust pan. She did it alright, put that mouse in the trash bag, and then we double-bagged it, took it outside, and set it on the grass for the trash truck to pick up. We did not kill it—we were brilliant and thought our conscience would be clear if we didn't smash the mouse and instead just let it suffocate and die in the bag.

Well, Mighty Mouse wasn't ready to die. I guess he was able to grip the grass and pull himself off the glue trap. Then he bit a hole in the bag, and next thing I know he was running through the grass and under the cars. My neighbor saw him and began to chase him to try to kill it; he said if we didn't then of course it would only go right back into the house. The neighbor went back and forth with that thing for a few minutes before finally catching and killing it.

My final experience was later, in one of the townhouses we lived in. By this time I knew the difference between the types of mice: the field mice are a green brownish color, and the city mice are gray. I learned that it doesn't matter how clean or neat your house is, when the temperature drops the crickets and the field mice will try to get inside, I guess to stay warm. I tried my hand at another set of glue traps, but this time I made arrangements with Jake, Tiffanie's friend, that when a mouse got on the trap he had to come right away. The agreement was fine. Everyone in the house knew the drill. Jake told me to put something on the trap to lure the mouse, so I put a piece of chocolate on it. The traps were in the kitchen next to the trash and the refrigerator.

Well, one night we were all in the bedrooms upstairs on the third level when suddenly Tiff came running upstairs laughing and said, "Ma, come downstairs—it's a big mouse on the trap. It caught a big one!"

I said, "Tiff, stop playing," and told Amber and Britt to go and look.

Pretty soon the rest of the Three Stooges came upstairs laughing and Britt said, "No, Ma, for real, it caught a big mouse on the trap."

By this time I had called Jake and said, "The trap caught the mouse. Can you come over?" He was at work, and I told him, "It's going to stay right there until you get here. I will turn off the kitchen lights and won't go in there." What was I thinking—that the mouse was scared of the dark?

Jake said, "Okay, Ma, I will get there as soon as I can."

The Three Stooges were still standing there laughing, so I went to the kitchen. I was easing my way into the kitchen. I didn't want to look at this mouse. I didn't even want to hear it, so I had my fingers stuck in my ears. Well, as I turned off the light my smart, very intelligent son J said, "MA!" I looked, and guess who the big mouse was? J had stepped on the trap while trying to get to the refrigerator and the glue trapped him. I don't think his three sister clowns realized that the glue could have pulled off his skin if it was snatched off of him. I told the Three Stooges to help me get him off.

So there I was easing the glue strip off my son. Now will someone please tell me why all the new homes have the air vents in the floors instead of in the ceilings like the old houses? Well, I went to move back a little and the heel of my $800 Gucci boot got stuck in the air vent. This is just my luck. Now we've got freaking mice in the house, my son is stuck on the mouse trap, and I'm stuck in the air vent. And can you guess what the Three Stooges were doing? They were all rolling on the floor laughing so hard they couldn't even help us. Today I can laugh about it, but at that moment I was so furious with them. You could have seen my face turn red, and my blood pressure shot right up. Larry, Moe, and Curly finally helped me extract my foot from the boot so I could help J. I was on one side of the kitchen, and there was my boot on the other side standing up stuck in the air vent. I did finally get J off that glue strip and sent him upstairs to take a shower and wipe the glue off of him. Then I had to lift the entire vent up off the floor and take my boot out. Mind you, I took my time because I was not going to break my heel. I also put the Three Stooges out of the house because they had gotten on my nerves so bad … I can now get another laugh from the memories!

The weirdest thing is once you are mad at someone you start thinking of everything else along the same lines. Well, this brought me back to the day my Three Stooges pulled another prank on J. Poor J—he lives in a house full of women and takes everything they throw at him like a trooper. Although his sisters are constantly smothering him and showing their love, they truly know how to get on his nerves. One day everyone was at home; the kids were down on the second floor while I was up on the third. When I came downstairs I saw J sitting in the corner on the floor. I thought that was very strange because we had the sofa and love seat in the family room. I asked him, "What's wrong?" In a sad little voice he said "nothing" while shaking his head no. I repeated, "J, what's wrong?" Then I noticed Tiff and Britt were in the kitchen laughing but keeping it in so J would not be able to hear them. I asked him the third time, "J, what's wrong?" This time he said, "Ma, I don't want to get in trouble. The police is going to come here."

At that point I called Tweedle Dee and Tweedle Dumb in the family room. Well, it turned out they'd tricked J with this ring tone that used comedian Steve Harvey's voice. Tiff dialed the number and gave J the phone, and he heard Steve Harvey yelling. If I remember correctly the ring tone went like this: "Hello? Hello? Who the hell is this?" J hung up and told her, "You dialed the wrong number," so she dialed it again and gave him the telephone. Steve Harvey was mad and said, "Who is this calling my house?" J was talking to Steve, saying, "I'm sorry, sir, I dialed the wrong number. It's the wrong number," and Steve was just yelling. Of course J didn't know it was a recording, a one-way conversation. Steve was not letting him talk; he just kept talking at the same time while J was trying to explain himself. J dropped the phone and said, "Tiff, we are gonna get in trouble. The police are gonna come! It's against the law to call celebrities' houses—you're not supposed to call them. The police are gonna come!" As fate would have it, at that very same time you could hear police sirens driving by on their way to another place.

It took me a while to convince him it was not Steve Harvey but just Tiff and Britt being silly—it was a recording he was talking to. I had to call all the way to New York to let J speak to my cousin Jas and have her tell him she has the same thing on her phone. We had to let him listen to Jas's ringer, and she told him she would beat Tiff up for him if she didn't leave him alone. I was so furious with them for doing that to him. Again, it's something we later laugh at. I'm laughing out loud as I write. I remember one day chatting with my girlfriend Tonia Davis and her saying, "Tinge, I bet it's never a dull moment in your house—your kids are too funny and they get it from their mama." All I could say is thank God laughter is good for you.

And Sarah declared, "God has brought me laughter. All who hear about this will laugh with me."
Genesis 21:6

Chapter 17

In Loving Memory of Mrs. Caroline S. Singleton
June 18, 1927 – January 28, 2005

⌒

My grandmother was a person that would open her house up to anyone in need. She had her very own personal food kitchen and lived in an apartment where she raised all eight of her children (two of whom preceded her in death) until there was a fire that burned out the entire building. She lived right next door to her sister Harriet and one floor down from her sister Amelia. My great-aunt Amelia died in her sleep, may God rest her soul. Amelia was the person that gave me the nickname "Tinge" the day my mother brought me home from the hospital.

Despite all the good things my grandmother did for others, she was never really a grandmother to me when I was growing up; in fact, she would never give us any gifts. I don't mean to paint my grandmother as a bad person, but I will tell you she didn't teach her children any values. I watched them all find their own paths. My grandmother never even finished elementary school, and I guess the only values she could teach were the ones she knew. She was a wonderful cook and always opened her home to whoever needed sheltering. She did give me one spirit, and later in life I found out that I had an approval addiction. I gave and gave just to make others happy. This is how I ended up spending so much of my money on others when I was older, which eventually bankrupted me. She argued about money with my grandfather all the time, so much that I remember thinking I never wanted to let money get me that way. That was why, even if I knew I shouldn't give someone money, I would do it just for the sake of avoiding an argument.

Now that I am older and understand a lot more than I did back in the '80s, I realize that my grandmother was addicted to prescription medicine. Since none of us knew it was an actual addiction, we never got her any help. There were times when she would act sick just to go to the hospital so that she could get a prescription. There were times that I know my uncle Butch most likely got prescriptions for her. There were times when my cousin strung out on drugs would get her prescription medication just to get money from my grandmother so she could go get drugs for herself. The day my grandmother went into the hospital after having a stroke, my aunt Valerie went through her room so that we could tell the doctors what medication she was on. That was the day the confirmation was made that she was indeed addicted to prescription drugs. My family found around fifty different prescriptions, most of them in other people's names.

After I moved away, my kids would go to New York every summer to stay with my mom since I worked so many hours. During this time they became close to my grandmother. We also had a family ritual that every New Year's Eve had to be brought in with Grandma and then you could go party or do whatever it was you wanted. We would all get together as a family, all the daughters, sons, grandkids, nieces, nephews—her entire family—and we would cry and thank God that we lived for another year. That was always emotional, and although we would all say we were not going to cry, there was always someone in the group that would start boo-hooing and we would all lose it.

When my grandmother had her stroke and was in the hospital, her great-grandchildren (Tiff and Britt) and grandchild Sade (Fufu) would visit her every day. It became really touching because Tiff took it hard and would not want to leave her. We would literally have to make her leave, and then she could walk back up to the hospital again the following day.

My grandmother was taken from the hospital to a nursing home, where her condition worsened. There were at least two different false alarms in which she was transported from the home to the emergency room and they thought she would not make it through the night. It got so bad that, as bad as it is to say, I was ready for her to go home with her father just so she would not suffer anymore. She caught an infection and her temperature was so high they ended up draining fluids from her brain. But God still was not ready for her. She was sent from the hospital to a different home. At this point my grandmother could not move, speak, or eat; she was being fed through a tube in her stomach. It was a very emotional time. One day all "H-E-double-hockey-sticks" almost broke loose because my grandmother was found on the floor of the home and my aunts and mom were not having it. They finally got calmed down, but we still don't know to this day if someone pushed her out of the bed or if she tried to get up and fell out of the bed. I guess only God knows, but that was a fighting moment.

Grandma was rushed back to the hospital one last time. I was in Maryland when I got the call from my mother that they wanted to operate on my grandmother's brain because she had a brain aneurism and they didn't think she would make it through the night. They needed permission from the kids to operate. Well, no one wanted to make the call. They were all at the hospital—her sons, daughters, great-grand- and grandkids—but not one person would make the call. It became my mother's responsibility because she is the oldest child. I told my mother to pray and leave it up to God. The family decided not to do the operation. Grandma made it through the night and her fever broke. To everyone's surprise, the machines were not showing the signs of a headache; the doctors said she should have been in excruciating pain but everything looked normal. God wasn't ready for her yet. About a week later she was transferred back to the care facility and her life was the same, lying in a bed, being fed through a tube. However, the family did not miss a day of being there to talk to her and let her know somebody was there. My uncle Justin would not go up to see her; no matter how bad it was, he wouldn't go visit her in the hospital. He told me he didn't want to remember her that way.

In the middle of the night of January 28, 2005, my mother called to tell me that Grandma was gone; she had died in her sleep. When I got the phone call I had to think about how I would tell Tiff and Britt. It was a terrible moment filled with emotions and feelings. I knew Tiff had an exam to take in the morning, so I chose not to tell her right at that moment. I waited for them to go to school, and after they returned home I explained to them that God needed Great-grandma, she is not suffering anymore, she's able to walk around on her own, and she will always be there to look over them.

The next day I found my uncle Justin and told him. He cried like a baby on the phone. I believe most of it was because he never went to visit her in the hospital. I told him we had to go up to New

York; everyone else was there already. Of course my uncle did not have a suit to wear, so I took him to the store and had them customize a suit for him and bought him a shirt, tie, and a pair of shoes. His friend was driving up to the funeral, so I rode up with the two of them. The arrangements for the viewing were beautiful. My uncle Skeeter worked at the funeral home and made sure everything was done top-notch. My grandmother was in a light pink dress and looked so young and peaceful. He really paid attention to the detail of how her wig was positioned. Grandma always wore wigs and was so stylish with it. She bought the most expensive one with the best of qualities. Grandma would be at home and would send her wig on its wig head out to the hairdresser to get it washed and styled. I guess back then that was the version of what we call weave.

The funeral was standing room only. The funeral home was not big enough, and people were standing outside the doors. We saw so many people that my grandmother helped, fed, and gave shelter to over the years. Everything was going okay until my uncle Justin showed his behind. Every time someone would speak, he would holler and try to get up out of his seat. The first time it was "Mommy, why, why, why?" Uncle Skeeter sat him back down. My uncle did a silent cry with his mouth open for a good thirty seconds without making a sound. My uncle Tony sat next to him and was elbowing him and pinching and poking him in his ribs. Then this man fell out on the floor in front of my two aunts Sheila and Valerie. They looked at each other and said, "We not picking him up." Uncle Tony told him, "Get your big ass off the floor." He kept hollering that he missed his "muva" (not "mother"). They told him to shut up. They were holding him by his collar so of course if he tried to move away he would get choked. It finally reached the point where Millie, my brother's aunt, just sat right next to him. Millie said, "Don't worry about him. I got this—he's not going anywhere." She told him, "You better pull yourself together and stop acting like an ass." He also yelled out that he and my grandmother look alike. "We look just alike," he yelled.

Then as the home going continued my uncle got up and walked over and leaned over the casket. My mother and aunt told him to sit down before he knocked the casket over. By this time Skeeter grabbed a chair to sit next to him. I was on the aisle across from him and noticed this man had on white tube socks and had a do-rag on his head. I was ticked off at that point; I just spent all this money and he couldn't even buy himself a pair of dress socks and get a haircut.

Once again for the second time he decided he wanted to run up to the casket and try to lean over my grandmother. By this time my uncle Tony, who'd been holding it together the entire time, lost it. He went in front of him, kneeled down, and told him, "If you get out of this chair one more time I am going to whoop your ass—it's gonna be me and you. You're sitting here making a scene—where were you when she was sick and in the hospital?" He said one grown man to another, "Get out this chair one more time and watch what I do." Needless to say, Skeeter didn't have to sit there anymore because my uncle Justin never got back out of his seat. He really made a scene. We can laugh at it now, but we were really mad and it was embarrassing back then.

My two daughters Tiff and Britt were so brave. Tiff wrote two poems for my grandmother, and she and Britt each read one. Everyone in the room was crying. My uncle Tony went up to stand next to them just to help them get through the reading of it. Tiff's poem ended up being placed on the back of the eulogy.

My uncle Tony also had an emotional moment trying to get through the reading of the eulogy. He did it though. And after all that he did at the funeral, my uncle Justin didn't even go to the after past; instead he just disappeared and went back to Maryland.

Grandma was cremated. I purchased urns and necklaces with Grandma's ashes for the family. Tiff wears hers around her neck at times, and Britt keeps hers on the rearview mirror of her car. She says Grandma is watching over her and before her track meets she always talks to her and gives her a kiss before going in.

Chapter 18

Trust in God, Not in Man

⌒

When it seems too good to be true, it really is too good to be true.

I learned a hard lesson in 2006. This was another lesson about listening when God is trying to get a message across to you, and this time it cost me $5,000. I'd been befriended by a man named Charlie. I had come to trust this man. I trusted him so much I let him borrow my BMW 645 convertible on several occasions when he told me his boss, Councilwoman Catherine, wanted to use it in a parade. I also handed over $5,000 cash to him so he could get me access to the deeds on two pieces of land I wanted to purchase. Charlie told me he knew people in the tax office and that I could purchase the property without having to attend the normal auctions. Here I thought I could go right to the source and didn't have to wait on line like all the others. I thought I was getting the hookup of the century. I was getting a great deal, or so I thought. I didn't have any reason to doubt him; I met him at his actual work location a couple of times so I knew he really worked there. But you've heard the saying "If it sounds too good to be true, it probably is"? Well, this was one case where that saying applied. I definitely had this feeling of misgiving that I now know was God trying to warn me off this deal. Unfortunately, I chose not to listen.

Charlie drove me out to show me the property. He also drove a friend of mine out to look at another piece of property, but it turned out to be the wrong address and that property had actually already been sold. This should have been another red flag. Of course I ended up not owning either piece of property. I did eventually realize I'd given up thousands of dollars to this man and had nothing to show for it. Another district attorney's office contacted me about it, but since it was a cash transaction I decided not to follow through with a lawsuit.

God takes care of things, though. The following year, Charlie was placed on administrative leave from his job as council aide in the councilwoman's office. According to Channel 8 and Channel 7 news reports, he was accused of writing fraudulent checks and a warrant was issued for his arrest. The checks were written from an account belonging to a charitable organization a former Washington Redskins football player established and Charlie was involved with. The complaint against him alleged that Charlie stole $15,000 from the charity. I don't know whether they ever got any of that money back. I certainly didn't get any of mine back, but I did learn that you'd better listen to God's warnings and not put your trust in man. At the end of it all I realized Councilwoman Catherine didn't have a clue that he was using her name to receive favors and special treatment.

Although I was very angry and felt violated that something I worked hard for was stripped away from me, I realized and I knew the only thing I could do was forgive him because Charlie is going to have to answer to God. It is public record how he used people and an entire foundation to get what he wanted. I am proud to give this situation to God because all Christians know I had to forgive him and turn it over to God. Vengeance is his, not mine, and the battle is not mine, it's God's. You see, for what Charlie has done he will have to answer to God, and I would hate to be in his shoes on judgment day.

Chapter 19

It's Always Something

I've been in the car business for fifteen years now, and some of the things I've seen you just would not believe. There surely is some money to be made. When I first realized how much it was possible to make, I decided I'd be a multimillionaire before I was forty. I'd have a chain of dealerships in different states and would travel by my private jet to visit them all. That was the dream, but before I could get there I'd have to deal with rude customers, obnoxious bosses and coworkers, drugs in the workplace—you name it, I've probably seen it at one time or another.

I remember working in one car dealership where at closing time the managers would all get beer and alcohol and play poker for money right in the conference room until all hours of the night. That went on for a while until one of the new employees got ticked off and called the corporate office about it.

There was so much sex and drugs in the car dealership you would not know who was a druggie and who wasn't. We all covered for one another and took care of each other, which was why we were one of the most profitable dealerships in our company. Everyone knew who was sleeping with whom—it was a huge soap opera—but we never spoke of it and never let anyone know that we knew about it. That was such a memorable time.

I only remember one lady being fired because she blatantly came to work high and couldn't function. The scary part was that she drove herself to work. She was so high on heroin that she was eating pretzels and leaving a staggering trail of crumbs wherever she walked. Those crumbs were everywhere, even in her hair. The worst part was that we were all so busy we didn't realize her condition until she was talking with a customer and nodded off to sleep. The customer got up furious, saying, "I'm not letting this f*%#*&% junkie help me! Get her the f%#& away from me!" When we all went into the room we immediately had her removed and driven straight to take a random drug test. Guess what? She beat the system. We later found out that she'd had a fresh perm put in her hair and the chemicals covered up the hair strand and made the drug test unreadable. So she got away with it that time, but the next time she came to work high she ended up getting fired. I later heard that while she was working at another dealership she nodded out and busted her head open from hitting the table. I also heard on another occasion she totaled her personal car because she nodded off behind the wheel.

That wasn't the only time I worked around a bunch of high-paid addicts. This one guy, you could set your watch by the time he went to lunch every day. Funny thing was, he never actually ate anything. Everyone knew he was on cocaine, but no one did anything—all he would do was deny it. I'm sure he was only in his late forties or so, but he looked like he was in his sixties. One time he went to the bathroom and when he came back out and started talking to me he had all this white powder on his face. I told him straight out, "If you don't get in that bathroom and wipe your face...." Then I was holding a conversation with him one day and his nose just poured with blood. He didn't even know he was bleeding because he didn't have any feeling left in his nose. Another time we actually saw him make his buy from a car parked outside the dealership gates. We couldn't identify who he was buying from, but he came back very hyper and could not keep still. That sort of thing just doesn't make any kind of sense. This man was literally disappearing before our eyes and no one could stop him.

I have also dealt with racism on the job. This one guy would always say things like "you people" or "you know, the black girl." We made him so uncomfortable. Whenever I would hear him say those words "you people," I would repeat it back to him, "you people" or "the black girl," and he would just try to laugh and say, "You know what I mean...."

Things were really crazy back when I first got into the car business. They didn't do background checks or drug testing then. Or if they did, I don't know how so many people were able to pass. We had this one sales guy that was a waste. He had so much talent and could sell cars at a minimum of twenty per month, and that was a lot considering there were twenty other salespeople. Well, this guy was a crackhead, and we found out that he was stealing cars from somewhere, he stole customers' down payment money, and even stole cars from the dealership. If someone wanted a car, he would meet the customer away from the dealership and sell it to them. He somehow got tags for these cars as well. It all finally came out when a customer came into the dealership mad as heck. He'd been stopped and nearly arrested because of the tags on his car. Well, when he came in to speak with us it turned out the sales guy was so good he had been taking monthly payments from people and giving them actual written receipts. This customer came in with all of his receipts. Wow. They gave this guy a chance at rehab, which he never completed, and they eventually fired him. The receipts had nothing linked to the dealership; the customer said they would always meet outside when he gave the salesperson the money. So we couldn't press any charges against the sales guy.

Another sales guy was a swinger. The worst part was that he actually ended up getting married and his wife never knew about his other lifestyle. He would tell us all of his stories, how he had a good friend that was a lesbian and the only way you could get in was if you were a couple. He would take this friend and act like she was his woman. He said while they were into their couples things—you know, all of them together—he would be having sex with the man's wife and his friend would also be having sex with her because she wasn't interested in the man. We would see him going to the Eckerd across the road to buy his K-Y jelly, and he would be psyched. He told us how he shaved all of the hair off his body. How his wife didn't know about any of this because he took the other girl. Well, three or four of the guys loved listening to his stories and decided to go with him. He would travel to Philadelphia; apparently these parties were very elite and would be in different locations. A couple of the guys ended up losing their marriages because they got hooked on swinging.

Another young guy, stupid as he was, took pictures high out of his mind with a girl passed out on a chair with a table full of cocaine in front of him. The pictures were sent around to everyone. He then met a different girl in a bar and went home with her and her friend and did a threesome with them. The poor fool married this girl after knowing her less than a month. He went through hell. His new wife had a baby daddy that was abusive and used to stalk them.

He would come to work with bloodshot eyes or sometimes wouldn't even show up at all. Well, he bought them a house and the wife got pregnant. I left the dealership, but when I later saw this guy he had lost a good fifty pounds. I asked him what was wrong with him. We were all like family and could talk to one another. Well, he told me that after he took care of this baby for about a year it turned out it was not even his child; his wife had slept with some repairman. I don't know why he was so surprised that he was having to get a divorce.

I myself was not exempt from the craziness. I didn't do any drugs, but before I got strongly into the church I did my share of what they call booty calls. I didn't want a relationship after separating from my husband, but those needs hit me from time to time and I wanted to be with someone. There was this one guy I worked with ... we spent so much time around each other and worked so much there was never time to go out and meet people. My twisted thinking was I had money, I could buy myself whatever I wanted, and I didn't need a man. Well, I slept with one of the guys. I didn't think he was all that attractive, but he had a way about him that made him think he was a gift to women. I went to his house maybe twice. I would go after the kids went to sleep. This was back in 2003 when I was staying at my sister's house. The first time I drank a beer or two so it made me think the sex was pretty good. I went back for a second time. The only thing was it was hard trying to do a booty call and then get back home. He wouldn't want me to leave, and I had to be back before my kids woke up.

This one night on my way home I was stuck in traffic and found out there was a terrible crash and traffic was stopped so that the medivac helicopter could land on the highway and pick up the patient. I sat there for about two hours, certain I must have dozed off a couple of times. Right then I knew that wasn't the life for me. And I couldn't just sleep with a man with no strings attached.

I've told you about all this stuff that can go on in some dealerships and with the people who work in them and haven't even mentioned the customers yet. I once sold a car to a woman who I would swear was bipolar. One minute she was the nicest person, then the next minute she wanted to rip everyone's head off and apologize in the same sentence. Those of you in the retail business will know exactly what I am speaking about when I say "retail customer from hell." To make a long story short, when she purchased this SUV I gave her everything she asked for, new tires and all—even though the car passed Maryland state inspection I gave her the tires anyway. She also wanted me to buy her a cover for the spare tire that was on the back of the SUV, and I told her no. I do try to please every customer, but I have come to the realization that I will not be able to do that. The thing is, when you say no to someone their head starts to spin. This woman was buying a car about six years old and she wanted to buy it like it was brand new, not taking into consideration the years of wear and tear and how it was considerably cheaper than a new vehicle. She proceeded to threaten the dealership, saying that she would call the news station, she wrote letters of complaint, and she would call the dealership about ten times a day. I don't know if she actually contacted the news station, but no reporter ever called or showed up with a bunch of cameras. This woman knew that I treated her fairly; she just didn't want to admit it. Finally she went away and I didn't hear from her for a while.

Then one day I was totally surprised when this same woman walked into the dealership and announced that she wanted to buy a car. I told her, "You are kidding me, right?" and she said, "No. I want to buy a car. Which one can I get?" I responded by saying, "Ma'am, considering the way things happened here the last time when you said you were treated so horribly, WHY are you here? Out of all the dealerships in the area, why did you come back here?"

She said, "Because I want to buy a car and you have nice cars."

I flat out told her I would not sell her a car. "You were irate the last time you were here, and I have no idea on this green earth why you would even come back here. I have the right to refuse a sale, and I choose to exercise that right today. Now please leave."

By this time one of the salespeople had come over. The customer told him, "I got money, I have a good job, and she's telling me she won't sell me a car."

I said, "Exactly, and I have no idea why you would want another car from people that were so horrible to you." Of course she proceeded to talk loud and then went out the door angry—and without buying a car. It turned out I was the one that was able to get her approved when no one else could.

I guess I will never understand what makes people think that if they cuss and fuss they can get what they want, especially when I have been treating them nicely from the start. Some people talk and say about me, "And she calls herself a Christian." I hear that every time I stand firm. What these worldly folks do not understand is that God didn't make us to be spineless punks; we have to take care of ourselves and know how to stand our ground. People often mistake my kindness for weakness, and it does nothing but surprise them when I have to show out. Trust me, I show out the Christian way. When someone is upset I still speak to them nicely, and that makes them even madder. Funny how I don't let them take me out of my element and it burns them up. I tell them they are not worth me blocking my blessing; I will pray for them and keep it moving.

Chapter 20

Best Friends Forever

My best friend, Cheryl Giles, is a very wise and Godly woman. She has a saying, "God didn't raise us to be punks, to get run over and taken advantage of," and she always follows this up with "Help me, Lord, I ain't got no sense. I got a fighting spirit."

Cheryl and I met in 2006 through a mutual friend. I sold her a car, and this woman became my BFF and the true sister I never had. Cheryl is the kind of friend who will always pray with me and for me. She knows everything I have gone through, both financially and with my family, and often she has discernment in different situations even when I am blind.

Now our families share Thanksgiving and Christmas dinners, usually with her pastor there too. We also have barbecues together, and whatever we do, we all chip in on the food because none of us could afford to feed everyone on our own.

I am so grateful that God has placed Cheryl in my life. With her, I can talk about anything and everything, and she has prayed me through more than a few rough spots, as you will see.

Chapter 21

The Car Dealership
(This was not the actual name of the dealership)

～

Things were so good when Jacob and Dennis first asked me to come over to work with the Car Dealership. This was in the summer of 2007. The plan was that they would get another location that I and my crew would run while Jacob and Dennis stayed at the current location. But it never worked out that way. I ended up as general manager for the Car Dealership, working from 9:00 a.m. to 8:00 p.m. six days out of every week.

Jacob and Dennis were brothers, but they were so different. Everyone that came into the dealership or knew them would say that the younger brother had something on the older brother. Dennis, the older brother, was about six foot five and had a limp. I was told it was from a car accident he had been in when he was younger. He had very thin legs and arms. If you saw him from the front you would say he was skinny looking, but when he turned sideways he had the stomach of a woman seven months pregnant. Everyone used to call him the Godfather because, although he was from a different country, he carried himself like an Italian man. He always stood and spoke with authority in his voice. Even if he was lying, his well-dressed appearance would make him believable.

Jacob was the younger brother, around the same height as Dennis, but Jacob was the laziest man I had ever seen. He always came into work after 1:00 p.m., and when he walked through the door he wouldn't speak, he would actually wait for you to speak to him first. I was taught growing up that when you enter a place, out of respect you should address the person already there; for some odd reason he thought it was the opposite. When he got there he would eat his lunch and go to sleep. One night he made me so mad. Jacob was still sleeping on the sofa in his office at 8:00 p.m., time for me to leave. I locked the front door to the dealership and went home. The next afternoon when he got in he said, "You just left me," like I did some horrible thing. Excuse me, is it my job to wake up Sleeping Beauty? I told him, "I called you a couple of times and you wouldn't wake up so I left."

And boy, Jacob would have on so much cologne. One time he walked in and stood next to me and I literally choked from the smell. I had to go get some water, and people were patting me on the back so I could breathe.

Jacob's wife and kids liked to hang around the dealership too. The kids would come like it was a playground; they would have toys all in the showroom and babies crying and making noise. You could see the frustration on the customers' faces. One day I'd had enough. I could not take any more. I said, "This is a place of business, not a daycare, and I'm not going to be stepping over toys and playpens to get to where I need to go to do my work." His wife's response was "I don't see what the big deal is." People would often come in and voice their opinions about the kids being there, but I couldn't do anything about it because they were the owner's kids. Once when I returned to the dealership after taking my son to the doctor's office, one of the salesmen, Jeff, told me that the little girl was running around so much she ran into the glass door and busted her nose open. He said he was scared because he never saw so much blood come from a little girl.

Then there was Lenny, Dennis's childhood friend. Before I started working there I used to think Lenny was the father. He looked and acted like a seventy-five-year-old man—even had a bad hip and walked with a limp—yet he was twenty-five years younger than he appeared. Poor Lenny, he would get worked so hard, with four people telling him ten different things. He had a very nasty attitude with all the employees but could switch it off when needed in front of customers.

Before I came to the Car Dealership, if your credit score wasn't over 650 you could not buy a car there. But as general manager I brought second-chance financing to the dealership, and they went from making no money to tons of money when the market was good. See, I knew from personal experience that having some bad marks in your credit history didn't automatically mean you were an irresponsible person who didn't deserve a chance. I knew all too well how hard it is to build a good life from scratch or rebuild a life that's been broken, and as both a Christian and a savvy businesswoman I knew that giving people an honest chance is just the right thing to do.

I will close this chapter by saying the two brothers ran that dealership into the ground. They did it without integrity, without caring about the customer. Once you purchased your car and left the dealership, good luck with getting anything done. I had disagreements with them daily regarding this issue and nothing would ever change. I made it clear to them that I would not let them ruin the relationships and reputation I had built over the years of being in the business. They made promises to customers and would never keep them. It had become so bad that it reached the point where nearly every day I would get angry customers calling me at the dealership, sending nasty emails, coming into the dealership wanting to do harm to me because no one knew them; I was the one on the front line, the one that everyone looked to. We called the police so much they told us we should get a security guard. It was so frustrating because there were minor things they could have done to keep a customer happy and thereby gain more customers. It was as simple as paying off the customers' loans when they traded in cars, getting their motor vehicle hard tags in a timely manner and not waiting for the sixty days you're allowed in Maryland to expire, all of which was Jacob the lazy brother's work function at the dealership. Just taking the time to speak with customers and not letting them think you're avoiding them, speaking nasty to them. These things are all simple parts of daily customer service. I always wondered why the entire two years I worked there I didn't see any repeat customers even though the dealership had been in business for over fifteen years. That was very strange. But as I stayed there those two years it became evident to me why no one was returning.

Chapter 22

Tiff

⁓

This chapter is dedicated to my bishops.
Thank you for your prayers and support.

The greatest pain a mother can feel comes from seeing her child in pain. Tiff, my oldest, has had such a rough time with her health. Since the time she was around fifteen or sixteen years old we have gone from doctor to doctor and hospital to hospital. We have been in the emergency room all night up until 6:00 and 7:00 a.m. The entire family has been exhausted. Most times we would just go right outside the hospital and sleep in my Tahoe truck, or in chairs placed one in front of the other. I would be at work for twelve hours, and the minute I got home at nine in the evening I'd have to go right back out to the emergency room. This all started with Tiff always complaining that she had pains, but every time we went to see the doctor they could not find anything wrong with her. Tiff, bless her heart, worked full-time as an assistant in a doctor's office at the same time she was going to school.

This went on for about three years. It was hard on the kids and me, but of course Tiff had the worst of it. Every time we went to the hospital they would keep us there for hours and then end up sending her home saying nothing was wrong with her. The other kids got to the point that they didn't even want to go to the hospital because they thought Tiff was faking. For a while she thought she was going crazy because she was in so much pain and the doctors kept telling her nothing was wrong.

We were all tired. I also felt helpless, frustrated, and angry. We can only imagine how Tiff felt. She was getting depressed on top of everything else. They had her on so many different medications her nightstand looked like a mini drug store. All the different medications were a test for us, because although one thing was feeling better, we had to worry and constantly watch out for her well-being from the side effects, the worst effects being depression or hallucinations. The only thing that would help her body pain was steroids, but while they took away one pain, they caused another pain: migraines. All the side effects had become so bad that Tiff wouldn't take the medicine. She would rather suffer the pain during the day than be depressed or have migraines. How could anyone stand to see their own child choose to become susceptible to constant pain? But that is what I had to do.

Tiff learned how to manage her pain. She could not walk up the stairs in the townhouse. It hurt her when she sat up, and it hurt her if she lay down. It was as though her entire right side was stiff when she would try to walk. She had the same symptoms as a stroke victim; she could not move her right side. She would be so out of breath if she tried to walk up the stairs she would have to take one step at a time, placing her hand under her right knee and lifting that leg to the next step.

As a mother there was only one thing I could do, and that was pray. We knew God's will, not ours, was going to be done, but I begged him to give Tiff a moment of peace. I anointed her daily with oil. I kept a Bible opened to Psalm 91 in every room of my house. I anointed the entire house from all spirits that were not of God. Tiff was scared to close her eyes to sleep because the medication gave her bad dreams. I set up my chair and ottoman right next to her bed and many nights would fall asleep in that chair. She would be freezing cold even though the room was not, and I would have to wrap her up in blankets just like a baby.

We were fighting the unknown. Many nights I would lie prostrate on the floor, crying and praying and just asking for understanding and knowledge of what we were dealing with. I had a sick child at home and other kids to support and take care of. I prayed on a daily basis for renewed strength and for the wisdom to know what I should say or do to help her get through this. The only hope Tiff would have would come from seeing the faith in me and the God all over me. I didn't understand it, but I trusted God. My baby and my finances were under attack, but still I trusted God.

As a mother, what do you say to your child when he or she looks at you and asks, "Why is this happening to me? Why is God letting me go through this?" Well, at that point there is no more holding back tears; you are totally vulnerable. Tiff asked me that question and then saw me temporarily fall apart; the woman that was superwoman to her was suddenly lying next to her crying. But I picked myself up because this was not about me. I had to be there for my daughter. I looked her in the face, and the only words that would come to mind were "God is not going to put more on you than you can bear. Our paths are predestined, and what you are going through right now, he's going to use you to bring awareness and to minister his word to other patients and young women you will come into contact with. God loves you, and only he knows the reason you are where you are right now." We prayed and I anointed her head with oil. I knew that what I said was not what Tiff wanted to hear; she just wanted the pain to stop. I'm not sure if I chose the right words to say to her, but I will tell you that at that very moment I got a praying spirit in me that I never knew I had. I went before God and I prayed with heart and spirit. I felt like I was sitting right in front of my father having a conversation with him, and I asked him to please give me the strength and wisdom, the knowledge I needed to help my child through this.

On the day before Easter, Tiff went in for a colonoscopy—yes, another test. On this day, something never seen before happened to, of course, Tiff. The barium that is given for the test hardened inside her intestines. The pain was so great that at every touch to her body she would scream. She couldn't sit, couldn't stand, and it even hurt to lie down. She went through this pain until they finally decided to make a small incision just to see if they could see what was going on inside her stomach. I was exhausted. The only thing I could do was pray. I prayed for the surgeons, I prayed for Tiff, and I prayed and commanded the angels to go into the operating room and fill it with their presence; they would cover Tiff, protect her, and stand in the gap to block anything not of God. While I was in the waiting area the surgeon came back out to update me. The time changed over; it was now Easter Sunday. I was informed they would have to take her appendix out because some of the barium had seeped into the appendix.

I was so exhausted. Right at the time I thought I'd really run out of gas, I remembered reading the Bible earlier and I started thinking about Psalm 121:2-7. Jodi came to the hospital to check on Tiff, and at that very moment we all—Jodi, the kids and I—gathered around the hospital bed and held Tiff's hand. We interceded and cried out to God. We began praying and seeking God, believing for a healing. Seeing Jodi really lifted Tiff's spirit.

Since I was not going to be in church on Easter Sunday, I sent my tithes in along with an offering, believing in God for a miracle. I need you to understand I felt I could not go to God empty-handed; I was going to put something on it and show God I was believing in him for a miracle. I needed to plant an immediate seed for a right-now harvest. I was not going to stray from what I normally would do, definitely not at a time such as this when I really needed him. Some would say it was understandable if I didn't get my tithes in that Easter Sunday. Yes, I know it would have been okay to drop it off later; however, it was the offering I needed to be placed on the altar that very moment in the midst of the prayers being sent up on Tiff's behalf, right in the middle of corporate prayer.

The surgery was done and Tiff was still in pain. Because the barium was white it prevented her insides from being seen on x-rays. She had to pass the barium before they could even get an x-ray. Poor girl was on laxatives for a couple days. The kids would be with her at the hospital during the day, and I would go straight there after working a twelve-hour day. I would drive the kids home and then go back to the hospital praying that I didn't fall asleep behind the wheel, and thank God he covered me. I would sleep there, then get up in the morning and start the routine all over again. This went on for nearly a week. Only two things helped me to keep my sanity during this entire ordeal. First, every day on the way to the hospital I would pray and command the angels to go before me to stand guard and protect her. And the second thing was to listen to Kurt Carr's song "God Is a Healer."

My heart broke seeing Tiff trying to pass that barium. It was almost like passing stones. I would have to be brave and go into the bathroom with her and she would scream, while all I could do was rub her back. I couldn't imagine the pain and I couldn't do anything about it. She was on morphine, but we had them take her off of it because she was always doped up. The nurses tried to relieve me, but Tiff wanted her mother there. I think since I didn't let her see me cry it eased her just a little. This was such a hard time, and I became frustrated and angry because I didn't have any family there to come and sit with Tiff just to give me a little break. I have never gotten out of line with my mom and aunts, but this time I told them off a little. My mom finally came down and stayed with Tiff the night before she was released. Even having that one day of relief was a big help.

My father, stepmother, and stepsister went to visit Tiff one day while I was at work. She said it was the most uncomfortable feeling. I can imagine it was uncomfortable for all of them. She said my father only stayed for a few minutes and then left and never came back in. I told her, "At least they came."

My brother came to the hospital while we were all there. He was on his way to my father's house, but he had this girl with him wow. She would talk and would not hold her head up. At first I took offense that she was a little stuck up because he always acts like he's GQ. That turned out not to be the case though. Turns out she was severely cockeyed. None of us knew who she was speaking to when she looked at us. I do not mean any harm, it just surprised us all and I wanted to know how he wound up with her. Of course their visit was also short.

The doctors tried taking x-rays for a couple of days. I was told the barium made everything look like a white sheet of paper and nothing could be seen. At one time they feared that it had gotten lodged in her small intestine and they would have to cut part of her intestine out in order to clear the barium. How could something that is one in a million happen to Tiff? She finally was able to pass enough barium so that the x-ray could be done. Praise God they didn't have to remove her intestines.

It still wasn't over though. One day Tiff's leg swelled to the point that she couldn't bend her knee and she could barely walk. The first thought was maybe she'd been bitten by a tick and had Lyme disease, but we ruled that out because Tiff doesn't go around anyone's grass, especially not to cut it. Then we thought maybe she was bitten by a spider—a couple had gotten into the house once before—but that was also ruled out. Well, Tiff had to go back to the hospital and get more tests run, more blood drawn. She would get migraines so severe we had to keep the downstairs completely dark just to ease it for her a little. By this time I was tired of all the tests and no one finding out anything, so when we had to go to the emergency room again I took her up to Baltimore to Johns Hopkins Medical Center. They have specialists there. We sat in the waiting area for hours until her pain got worse and I became a frustrated mother. After I finished talking to the staff I told them I wanted all their names because I was going to report everyone in there. Tiff's head was pounding, her leg was swollen, and she had been sitting straight up in a chair for hours. Eventually to keep me quiet they put us in the family intercept room. This is the room they keep families in when the doctors have to deliver not-so-good news. It was eerie, but comfortable for Tiff.

By this time her neck started to stiffen up, and now it became serious. With all the symptoms she had, they wanted to test her for meningitis. No one could be around her until they confirmed whether or not she had it. I took the kids outside, and they slept in the car while I went back and forth to check on Tiff. They would let me go in but I had to wear a mask. By the grace of God she did not have meningitis. So they started another series of tests and blood work. Tiff ended up being admitted to Johns Hopkins for a couple of days.

We still didn't know what Tiff had. She was tested for lupus, sickle cell, meningitis, MS, HIV—every illness you can think of, and too many for me to name. Now they finally decided to do a biopsy on her leg.

The week before the biopsy, there was a healing service in the church. So many of the members, including the father of the house, were being attacked with different illnesses. I knew that I had to get Tiff to the church to be in the middle of what God was about to release over the congregation. When we got to the church I had my usual seat which was on the second row. That was okay for me and the rest of the kids, but for Tiffanie that was like a long walk up a very steep road. After getting her settled and after praise and worship it was time to do the altar call so that the ministers could pray and be in agreement for healing with you. Matthew 18:19: *Again I say to you that if two of you agree on earth concerning anything that they ask, it will be done for them by My Father in heaven.* Tiff couldn't even walk up to the altar; the men had to carry her. After the mother of the house prayed over her she told Tiff to walk around the church. Everyone was in tears, and by this time I was out in the spirit. Tiff started to walk around the church. Watching her was like watching a ninety-year-old woman in a twenty-year-old's body. Her steps and stride were very small, and she barely made it to the first corner of her journey of walking around the church. Well, Bishop, praying and worshiping through his very own pain and illness, went over to Tiff, picked her up, wouldn't let any of the other men help him out, and with tears rolling he carried her back to the altar, stood right in the middle of the altar and lifted her up to God praying. This was so emotional, but God covered the two of them with peace. The entire church prayed along with the bishops for order to be restored to her body, for her organs to function the way they are supposed to. The prayer was so powerful I lost it and blanked out, couldn't remember a thing. People all throughout the church were falling down filled by the spirit. What I saw after I was able to sustain myself a little was the inspiration and courage that was sent down to her. At that very moment Tiff knew she was not alone. She knew that God was with her; she knew she was surrounded by prayers and agreement for healing. I saw her spirits get lifted; I saw her facial expression change from worry to confidence that she would be healed.

After visits to many, many doctors and getting many, many tests, we finally had an answer. We knew what Tiff had. They called it reflex sympathetic dystrophy (RSD). From what I understand, RSD can happen when part of the body has been injured. RSD patients suffer unexplained intense pain that can be treated with steroids or morphine. They may also have swelling and loss of motion in the affected body part. Sometimes people with RSD have to get nerve blocks—an injection of anesthetic around certain nerves—to relieve the pain.

Ironically, a previous customer of mine had come into the dealership to see if he could trade the two cars he and his wife had purchased from me and buy one. He said they were no longer in a position to keep the two cars because his wife was very ill. When he told me she had the same illness as Tiff, I didn't believe it; I thought the doctors had made RSD up just for Tiff because they didn't know what she had. When this man's wife found out my daughter also had RSD, she had her husband drive her to the dealership to see me. She wanted to form a support group with Tiff. Just like with Tiff, there was a time this woman thought she was going crazy because she was in so much pain but the doctors kept saying nothing was wrong with her. She had to stop work because of the headaches, and she hurt so bad no one could hug her.

Tiff was on disability from her employer for almost a year. She also had a very hard time attending school. Every other week she would have to have a nerve block done on her leg and get a shot in the back of her head for the migraines. By God's grace she has been able to return to work full-time and she is now in her senior year of college nearing graduation. God can and will take control. He may not come when you want him to, but he will be there right on time. I prayed for peace and for Tiff to be able to sleep without pain. God on his time saw fit to bless her so that she can be a blessing to others. Now when she is at work and someone is in the doctor's office she tells them she knows how they feel and has the scar to show them. Tiff is very involved with the church she attends, she accompanies me and handles all the arrangements for the different speaking engagements, and she has put together her very own foundation named Waggy Mentoring that helps young men and ladies who are placed into the juvenile prison system. She is set on giving back to the community and trying to make a difference in someone's life, among so many other things. If you'd like to send Tiff an e-mail to learn more about her foundation, you can send it to info@waggynow.com or visit her website at waggynow.com.

Chapter 23

Be Careful Not to Become What You Dislike

At one time I really had to make a huge adjustment in my life in order to save my family. When you go through so many heartaches, one disappointment after the next, I believe regardless of how strong you think you are, sooner or later you will be touched. I know I was.

I am a Christian and one hundred percent faith believer. I know that God changes things, I know that God's will is going to be done and not mine, I know that he will not put more on me than I can bear, and I know that my timing is not the same as God's timing. I also know that Satan likes to divide and conquer. Even knowing all that and so much more, I did not see an almost fatal train wreck coming; I nearly had a head-on collision.

My father was never affectionate to me. I can't remember ever hearing him tell me that he loved me, not once. If I received a hug from him, it was always without any love or feeling to it—you know the one, the kind of hug that you give someone as you meet them just to say hello.

I know that what I am about to say is a strong statement to make. When I was growing up I used to really love my stepmother so much. I felt that she really cared about me even though I was not her biological daughter. As an adult I grew to understand my childhood feelings did not reflect reality.

When Sylvester told me and the kids to leave his house, Sharon stood right there and didn't say anything, didn't put her foot down at all. I went back in time and realized that throughout my entire childhood I learned the very same treatment from her as from my dad. Do you remember as a child if you were in a room with two adults and you fell down you would look at the adults to see who would come to your aid and comfort you? Those were my feelings and it didn't happen. My stepmother was just as bad as my father. If my dad stops speaking to me, then Sharon stops speaking to me; if my dad wants to be around us, then Sharon wants to be around us. If my dad buys Christmas gifts, we get them; if he doesn't, we don't. I had to repent and ask forgiveness because I came to the conclusion that the reason I loved Sharon was because I hated Sylvester. I will say it over and over again: My dad didn't hug me, my father never made me feel comfortable around him, my dad never said he was proud of me or that he loved me. Neither did Sharon. What used to bother me so much was the fact that they always buy Christmas and birthday gifts for my stepsister's son and for my brother's son and now daughter as well as throw birthday parties for them, like those are the only grandchildren they have. It doesn't bother me anymore; now I just feel sorry for Sharon and my father. My children are all doing quite well, and my father and his wife have missed out on their wonderful experiences. My oldest daughter just received three college associate's degrees and is now working on her bachelor's. Brittney just returned from running track in Australia and is currently a part of her college track team. Amber and J are doing great things as well. These are the outcasts of the grandkids just as I am the outcast of the children. I can go on and on, but let's get back to what I was talking about.

The worst thing to come from that lack of affection was I would do the same thing without even realizing it. Britt and Tiff once told me I was starting to act like my father.

My kids would say they loved me and I would just say thanks. I was very big on hugging and giving them kisses, but the "I love you" part went completely over my head. That is, until one day my little son J made it very clear to me. I would always hear the kids tell one another "I love you." I would always hear them say it to me too. I guess I took it for granted that they already knew Mommy loved them. One day Jesurun went around the room and said, "Tiff, I love you," and she replied, "I love you, J." Next it was "Britt, I love you," and she said, "J-Reppin, I love you too." Then "Amby, I love you." Of course she was a little rough around the edges, so she replied, "Yeah, I love you too." When it was my turn, J said, "Mom, if I tell you I love you would you say it back to me?" I looked at my son and asked him what he meant. He said, "I always tell you I love you and you never say it back. You just give me a hug and a kiss. Ma, can you tell me you love me? I just want to hear it."

Even if you are not in church you can be filled with the spirit anywhere. I was so overwhelmed I told J I loved him very much. I couldn't help the tears that were falling. Imagine how bad it must have been for my daughters growing up and not hearing me say those words on a daily basis. I would say it and let them know when I was proud of them, but I never realized how important it is to say it and let them hear it every day. They never mentioned it to me, but my little man did. He was hurting and needed to know that I did love him.

I called my mother and told her I loved her. After I did that, she called my aunt Ann and told her she was really worried about me. She knew I was going through rough times, and because I said those words to her as our conversation was ending she thought the worst. She told my aunt, "Tinge never says 'I love you.' I am worried and need to go make sure she is okay."

Today I make sure I tell all my children I love them. Now when J says, "Mom, I love you," I tell him, "I love you more." You can buy your children every game in the world, all the clothes in the world, but with my kids "I love you" takes me a whole lot further. You see, my kids are ride-or-die kids—they stick right by my side through thick and thin. They didn't even think about leaving me to go stay with Grandma through all the down-and-out moments I've dragged them into. My oldest daughter Tiff once said, "Ma, we only have each other, nobody else. You do so much for everybody, but in the end it's only us."

I must also give thanks to Sharon, for it's because of her that I have a relationship with my stepdaughter Shavonna that no one can break. I remember going to Shavonna's high school graduation. She told me she loved me, and when I told her I loved her she said she wasn't sure if I was going to come to her graduation. I told her I wouldn't miss it for the world. I explained to her, "I divorced your father, not you." I remember being the stepchild, and I was not going to make her feel the same way my stepmother made me feel. She said she was even shocked when the kids called her "sister." She thought they would stop, but they too told her she will always be their sister.

I love my children, family, and friends. I will not take those words lightly and for granted anymore. God is love.

Chapter 24

First Ladies Awards

～

"Ask Shanise" gave me a marketing brand and made me well known all over the Maryland, DC, and Virginia area. This was one really positive thing that came from my association with the Car Dealership. Ask Shanise did the sponsorship for "That's My Story" on Praise 104.1 FM's *Matt Anderson Show*. Matt Anderson is an amazing radio personality, and through our sponsorship during his show I was able to brand my own name. The advertisement went like this: "That's My Story is sponsored by Askshanise is the general manager of the Car Dealership. Go Ask Shanise, 'Have You Seen My Keys?'" Now whenever people hear the name Shanise they automatically say, "Have you seen my keys?"

I sold cars to notable pastors, radio and TV personalities, along with people in the sports industry. God has placed so many people in my path, and I thank God each and every day for my many testimonies. The one bond that he has given me was that of a sister and brother, Sheila Stewart and her husband Pastor Bill. I first met Sheila when she was referred to me to purchase a car. That night she didn't just get a car but a friend and sister forever. The very first meeting when I sat with her we spoke like we had known one another for years. It was late in the evening and we were about to close. Sheila and Bill stopped by just to look, not even expecting to get a car. I ended up speaking to Sheila on the phone the next day. It was so funny because we did a speaker call and at the time there were two other people in my office: my pastor and another gentleman. Their first impression of Sheila was that she talks too much and they really didn't think she could do anything. Well not I. I give everyone the benefit of the doubt and trust people until they prove me wrong. Everyone that crosses my path gets treated the same way.

I finally sold the husband-and-wife duo a BMW X5 truck, but that was the day my life changed. As I was speaking with Sheila I told her my testimony. She said she heard of the wonderful things I was doing by getting loans for people who normally would not be able to get them, and I told her when you go through something and try so hard to think of ways to get out of it, you end up mastering it. I told Sheila I've had bad credit, I've had great credit, I've made a lot of money and known how it was to have no money, I have been homeless but by the grace of God was able to afford a hotel room for me and the kids, I have had a car repo'ed, had the sheriff's knock on my door to put us in the street, filed bankruptcy, and had a negative bank account. I told her that's why I do my best to work hard to get the loans approved. I told her I am a single mother of four beautiful children, I am very active in helping to raise funds for my church, and I donate and give back to the community whenever I can, both personally and through the companies I worked for.

When Sheila heard my testimony she nominated me for the First Ladies Awards in Business and Philanthropy. During all of the research it was discovered I was one of the first African American female general managers of a luxury car dealership in the state of Maryland. I have been in the business since 1994 and have had an active role in selling thousands of cars nationwide.

I was honored to accept the nomination, not just for myself but because of where some of the proceeds were going. Part of the money was going to a foundation that mentors teens and young adults on life's challenges, including diseases and sex. The foundation helps young people mature into responsible adults and prepares them to enter the work force. The second beneficiary was a home that houses single mothers with HIV and their children (in March 2009, Maryland was ranked in the top three nationwide for HIV infections). Single mothers needing shelter—that hit home with me, and I was overwhelmed with tears.

I had a prescheduled appearance which aired on My Voice DC/myfoxdc.com with hosts Wisdom Martin and Roz Plater. I also had scheduled interviews on Praise 104.1 FM's *Matt Anderson Show*. The day the interview aired on the radio, the founder of another organization came into the dealership just to say she heard my testimony and wanted me to work with supporting her organization

(I'll tell you about that later). My life changed when I met this sister. She took my heart to another level. Suddenly I realized there was so much that I had to offer just by giving my testimony. Truly, 2009 was turning out to be a momentous year for me. Of course "different level, different devil" is the saying. When you are about to be blessed the waters will stir. This was going on at the same time my oldest daughter, Tiff, was so ill. In fact, Tiff was hospitalized in Baltimore on the day I was scheduled for a photo shoot for the flyer advertising the First Ladies Awards event. I ended up having to use the camera on my cell phone to take my picture and send it over straight from the hospital.

The awards presentation was on the morning of March 14, two days before my youngest daughter, Amby, turned fourteen. It was held in Upper Marlboro, MD. It was a star-studded event attended by notable politicians, pastors and first ladies, radio personalities, the mayor, councilmen, NBA players, and quite a few of DC, Maryland, and Virginia's elite players. The nominees included twelve women and five men.

Many of my family members were among the more than four hundred attendees as well. My aunt Ann and cousins Jas and Sheka drove down from New York with their boyfriends, and my little cousin NuNu came along with them. My mother had come to town the Friday before (Friday the 13th). Quite a few of my church family also showed up, and even my dad, stepsister, and stepmother came to show their support (or so I thought). I really thought this was going to be a new start for me and my father.

Unfortunately, things got off to a rocky start with my father. I had a total of four tables full of supporters. My mom and kids were at the first table, with my church family at tables two and three along with my employees and best friend Cheryl and her mother. By the time my father and his crew arrived there was seating available at the third table. He came up to me as I was greeting my guests and said, "I don't know these people. We need to be sitting with the family" (meaning my mom and kids).

I told him, "These are all my friends and everyone is sitting together." He was ticked off. I told him, "Today is not about you, and I am not going to let you get me upset. Now let's take a picture." If you could only see that picture—it was me, my dad, stepmom, and stepsister, and I was the only one smiling. I was determined to be the light that shined around such darkness.

The awards started, and as soon as my father realized the caliber of people in the room and the many supporters I had, he started to walk around letting everyone know his daughter was getting an award. Joe Coleman from the legendary group the Platters was performing. I saw my father get out of his seat and take some pictures. I thought he was taking pictures of me, but he was actually photographing Joe.

After breakfast it was time to hand out the awards. Dr. Lonise Bias (the mother of the late great basketball star Len Bias) was the second speaker, and she went a little over time. None of us seemed to care though, because she is such an extraordinary woman. This mother lost two sons to the streets: College basketball great Len Bias died from using drugs for the very first and only time less than two days after he was drafted by the Boston Celtics, and his brother was gunned down at a shopping mall. We were all honored and blessed by hearing her give her testimony and speak about the foundation she has started.

Because Dr. Bias's comments had taken longer than planned, we were all asked to keep our acceptance speeches very short. As my turn came up I knew I had to put aside the two-page speech I'd prepared the night before and think of a shortcut. My speech went as follows:

"I would like to thank my four beautiful children whom I have missed so many holidays with and school activities with because of working fourteen-hour days six days a week. Tiff, Britt, Amber, and Jesurun, I love you all. I would like to say, Mom, I love you and you were my role model. You raised me a single mother all by yourself. Thank you so much. My aunt and my cousins drove down from New York. Aunt Ann, I have to say thank you for being my babysitter and helping raise me when my mother was working to support me. My cousins, this award is for us all. All my family knew was welfare and being single parents raising kids as we grew up. Well, I am here to break the generational curse off of us. We are going to be the working generation that moves us forward, and this award is not only for me but for all the women in our family. My father is here. My father and I have not seen each other for over three years, but today he is here and I hope we can go forward and continue to move on from here, right, Dad? My church family, you know you guys are my family, and thanks for supporting and helping me and the kids and being my family away from my New York family and not letting us feel alone. I have to ask one last person to stand, and that is my BFF Cheryl. I know I keep you on your knees praying because I am always under attack. I know when you see my number on the caller ID you say, 'O Lord, let me go pray.' But I have to say thank you so much for having my back."

The crowd applauded each time I asked my family members to stand and be recognized during my speech. Of course my mother and aunt were crying. This was a very proud and humbling moment for me.

Cheryl said that throughout the entire ceremony she felt this coldness sitting behind her. It was so disturbing she turned so she could see this man's face and not have her back to him. She just kept fighting his spirit. Her mother asked what was wrong, and she said, "This man behind me is not right. He has a darkness." Well, she found out that man was my father when I asked him to stand. She told me he has a spirit that is very jealous of me.

When we all went to mingle after the awards, I found out that my father had left because I offended him by saying I was raised by a single mother. He walked out and left my stepmother there too; she had to catch a ride with my stepsister who lived an hour away from her. Wow, I told the truth and shamed the devil! My stepmother made me so mad because as usual she was trying to plead his case saying, "Well, he did help you and let you move in with us." I got so ticked off I walked away. Had she forgotten this was the same man that locked the screen door and exited the rear of the house just so that my kids would not be able to use the key to get into the house after school because he kicked us out? You have got to be kidding me. I had to walk away from her. Who cares about him anyway? This was my mother's time to shine for doing such a good job with me. She was the role model that helped me to get there. My award was being dedicated to all the women in my family.

Chapter 25

Speaking Engagement

I had met Coressa back in March when she heard my testimony during a radio interview. She was very passionate, just as I was, and again I shared my testimony. My life is not mine; it belongs to God, and I will spread his word each and every time. All I need is just one person. I agreed back in March to come speak at an event partnered with Children's Hospital on Sunday, April 26.

On that day I had to fight back my tears during my message just so that I could get it out. Sheila and Pastor Bill came out to support me, along with my mother and the kids and my BFF Cheryl. I was one of the keynote speakers. The organization helps women who are victims of domestic abuse. They provide them with shelter, furniture, and on some occasions transportation. I only had five minutes to speak. This is what happened when I was introduced:

"I know everyone knows me as the Car Lady and Ask Shanise. People see me driving nice cars, and I may even drive a different car every day. People want what they see that I have. They think I have it going on. Some even think I'm bougey. Well be careful what you ask for, and definitely do not ask for what I have now until you are ready to walk in my shoes. You do not know what I have been through...." By now I was fighting back the tears.

I told them, "Ladies, this hits home for me because I have been homeless, my four kids and I have lived in a hotel for over a month not knowing where we would end up, I almost had my kids go into the system because of the school district where your kids could not be absent unexcused more than three days in a marking period. What the school didn't know was that I was driving them from the hotel over thirty minutes each way." I couldn't hold the tears back now because everyone else was crying.

"I have not been physically abused, but I know how it felt to be with a good-for-nothing husband. I had enough when my family had to send money for us to keep a roof over our heads and the sheriff was knocking on the door. So, ladies, when you see me standing here in front of you, yes, I went from not having a dime to now managing millions in lines of credit for the dealership. Yes, I drive Mercedes, Bentleys, and whatever car I want to because of my profession, but remember there was a time I didn't have a car at all. Those people that say they want to be me or have what I have, how dare they? Ladies, look at me and know you cannot have a testimony without first going through a test and, ladies, you are going through, which means you will not be staying in the place you are at no matter how it looks. Pray and trust God, have faith God is using me and he will call on you to tell others your testimony. Don't give in. I know where you are now because I have been there. I have to say, Coressa, thank you so much for an organization that can help. Thank you."

I never imagined I would become a motivational speaker. Back when the kids and I were living in that Red Roof Inn, I could not see how the Lord intended to take that situation and all the other trouble I went through and use it for good. Who would have thought that someday people would want to listen to my story, that my testimony could instruct or encourage anyone? But this is where God has placed me, and now every time I prepare to go out to speak I follow what the Lord places on my heart and say just that. I keep it short and just talk about where I came from throughout my life. I pray that it touches and changes the heart and mind of someone who may be just about to throw in the towel. I pray that their desperation and hopelessness will be turned into inspiration and hope, enough to let them understand that if God can do it for me he can do it for them too.

Chapter 26

In the Presence While History Is Being Made

~

This chapter is dedicated to Deunka Wade, Gerald Evans, and Ernest and Darienne Merchant.

I was the recipient of some powerful inspiration when, on April 28, 2009, I stood in attendance while history was being made at the United States Capitol Visitors Center, Emancipation Hall. Tiff and I were among more than 1,500 men and women specially invited to witness the unveiling of the Sojourner Truth statue. This was such an historical moment for me, and to have the chance to share it with my firstborn daughter was priceless. The National Congress of Black Women rallied to have Sojourner Truth placed in the Capitol, and after they were turned down several times, history was finally made on this day that God made.

First Lady Michelle Obama (looking just as beautiful in person as she does on television), Secretary of State Hillary Rodham Clinton (television does not do her justice—she also looked beautiful), Congresswoman Nancy Pelosi (she always looks so conservative on television, but her hair and clothes were exquisite), National Chair of the National Congress of Black Women Dr. E. Faye Williams, Esq. (I admire her dearly and there isn't a time that I am in her presence that she isn't flawless), Congresswoman Sheila Jackson Lee, Congressman Elijah Cummings, Yolanda Adams, Dawn Lewis, Alfre Woodard.... There were just so many people in attendance, too many to name.

I must say First Lady Michelle Obama gave a speech that will ring in the Capitol for many years to come. It was a huge honor to see her unveil the bust of Sojourner Truth. I was very surprised when Dr. E. Faye spoke and mentioned that it had been then-Senator Hillary Rodham Clinton that gave the final push to get the vote passed to authorize the statue. Mrs. Cicely Tyson performed "Ain't I a Woman." She looked like such an angel in person.

There was a time when women could not get into the White House, women were not even allowed to vote, and here I was in the room with a stage full of women in top positions of the United States government. It was awesome.

All of the leaders stayed around after the unveiling for a meet-and-greet moment. That was when Tiff disappeared. This little lady made her way right up to the stage and was able to get close-up pictures of First Lady Michelle, Nancy Pelosi, and Hillary Rodham Clinton. When she came back to our seat she was jumping up and down so excited that one of the news reporters came over and asked if she could interview Tiff. She wanted Tiff to speak as a young adult who was a part of history being made. All I can say is God, thank you so much for allowing the two of us to experience this memorable moment.

Chapter 27

Empowerment Temple Church

～

"My people are destroyed for lack of knowledge."
Hosea 4:6

May was women's month at Empowerment Temple Church with Pastor Dr. Jamal Bryant in Baltimore. Each Tuesday the church would host a guest speaker. The series was called *"Let the Sistas Light Shine."*

On May 19, 2009, the topic was "Know the Game: Smart Tips for Big Ticket Purchases." It was such a great honor to be asked by Empowerment Temple Church to come out and share my experience in the car business with the members. I had always heard so many things about the church but never had the opportunity to attend until that day.

I spent most of the day preparing. I put out an e-mail blast asking all the women to send me questions they would love to hear the answers for. The feedback was so huge it reconfirmed my thoughts that this was a very good thing to do.

There was only one issue, and that was that the owners of the Car Dealership didn't understand why I had to go. They even tried to get me to cancel. I had to explain to them exactly what I was doing, and then I refused to cancel and went anyway.

The treatment I received at the church was first-class from the very first moment I arrived. I was immediately escorted into Pastor's office, where I was given water and had time for prayer. My prayer is always thanking God for using me to represent him and for showing his greatness. I offer my appreciation for my testimony and add that I will be so grateful to the Lord if my testimony could make a difference for just one person.

I was so happy to see that a few of my church members had come. Ernest and Darienne Merchant, Lisa Ennis, and Donald Colbert were all there. It was great to have them there, and my four children sat in the front row. Seeing their familiar faces helped me relax. I was nervous. This church was huge! The men and women that attended were great ... but of course we always know there will be one troublemaker out of every bunch. I'll come to him in a little bit.

I'm not good at following a speech. I like to write notes so that I'll be sure to get my points across, but paper and I are no match when it comes to speaking engagements. Here's what I said:

"I give all glory and honor to God for allowing me to stand before you and not only tell you the paths I've walked down but give you an insight on the car business. My name is Shanise Craft and I am the general manager of a luxury car dealership. I started out in the industry in 1994. I have held many positions throughout a couple of dealerships and worked my way up to the position of general manager. I thought it would only be fitting to tell you briefly about myself. I am always told I am good at what I do, helping people with challenged credit. I know they consider me, quote unquote, a finance guru; I will tell you why. When you are in a mess that you are trying to get out of, you find plenty of time to try to master that very thing. I have learned from experience.

"Just because you have bad credit does not mean you are a bad person. When you do not know where your next place to live is going to come from, the last thing that will be on your mind will be a bill.

"I have walked down the very same paths that some of you are on this very moment. I am a single mother of four. Thank God they are very good kids. I'm very proud of each and every one of them, and they are beautiful. I know how it is to have a family that depends on you and for your heart to be broken because you can barely take care of the necessities, the needs, forget about the wants.

"I know how it is to decide I finally had enough and get divorced and leave without money in your pocket or a place to live. My kids and I stayed in a hotel for over a month, because sometimes family can be your worst alternative. I was offered by my father and stepmother to move up to Maryland, but when things didn't go his way the kids and I were put out by my very own father, their very own grandfather. We moved into a hotel before moving in with another relative.

"I know how it feels to file bankruptcy and to lose everything you have and to start over not knowing if you want to. I know what it is to pay high interest rates because of credit issues.

"I know how it is to let someone else use your credit (cosigned for) and then stick you with loans. Even though he was my husband.

"I know how to deal with repossessions because I have had repossessions.

"Yes, I am a female in a boys' club. I know, women, you think you get taken advantage of when going in to try to purchase a car. Well, try being there and right in the midst of it every day. I am tested/challenged almost daily by men, but it's always very sad when it's one of my sisters that thinks speaking to a man instead of a woman would be better.

"In Hosea 4 verse 6 it says, 'My people are destroyed from lack of knowledge.'

"When I was growing up I didn't have anyone to tell me about credit and how to purchase cars and houses. At that time my grandfather and grandmother had lines of credit. You know Mr. Warren that owns the store … we'd get what we needed and pay him once a month when the checks came in. The furniture store … that store owner would come to visit once a month for his payment…. Cars, forget about it. I didn't get my first car until I was twenty-four years old, and I had to get it by myself and was ripped off. They charged me twenty-eight percent, which depends on the state max rate, and because I lived in Georgia I paid it. Not only that, because I didn't do my research I purchased a car that was in an accident previously; the passenger door was like lifting weights to try to get it opened.

"Do I think women are targeted to be ripped off? That may be a stigma with me being a female, but I would say NO. We are not getting ripped off because of being a woman, it's because we like to play the damsel in distress. We depend on men to help us through the process; therefore we limit and block ourselves out of knowing what we need to know in order to handle the purchase and handle our own business.

"Know the game. Do the research on whatever car you want before you leave your house to buy. When you stand toe to toe with the salesman, the manager, or whoever it is, you tell them about the car. When you have knowledge of a product you will take away the control of the sale.

"Right now I am speaking from a side that no dealership would want you to hear. I will answer the questions you ask me. I know that as a dealer my goal is to sell you guys cars, but as a Christian I want to sell your entire family a car. That means that my service to you was so good that you trusted to send them to me."

As I said earlier, there is always one out of every bunch. We went over everything from maintenance, gap protection, financing, even extended warranties. I had one guy of course that kept trying to act as though I didn't know what I was talking about. He said that people shouldn't buy extended warranties on new cars. I told him, "Of course you should; if the manufacturers felt like nothing would ever go wrong with the car then they wouldn't put a limit on the amount of warranty you're given. If you purchase the warranty while it's under the manufacturer's warranty it will be cheaper, still considered as a new vehicle versus used."

Well, I went back and forth with him for a few minutes. Finally he said, "I used to be a salesperson." I recognized him. He did once work with me at a dealership in Baltimore back in 2003/2004, and he was not very good. At the time he was a salesperson I was the finance manager of the same dealership. Of course managers stayed and hung out with other managers and salespeople were with sales. So unfortunately he wasn't privileged to realize how knowledgeable I was about the business.

I told him, "Yes, I know you used to be a salesperson [I also knew his position never advanced past sales], but I run the dealership. So I'm sure that you can be safe to say I know what I am speaking about very well."

I tried to make it a helpful question-and-answer segment, and thank goodness for me the women there were just about sick of this guy trying to act like he knew what he was talking about. They told him, "Sit down. She already answered your questions and you keep asking the same question...." LOL ... It took everything in me not to laugh. However, I went there to share my knowledge of the car business, and many people there had great questions, so many I can't list them all. Bottom line is they wanted to learn and I had the expertise to share with them.

I must take this moment to say, Pastor Dr. Jamal Bryant, you were so inspirational to me, you are an anointed man of God. You, along with Nicole Kirby, took time out to come into my office and speak with me, to encourage me, and by all means I do not take that lightly. We spoke about visions and helping the communities. I will dedicate my talents and expertise to doing God's work. Thank you, Pastor Bryant. I know I went to speak and empower the members at your church; however, I walked away from your church empowered as well.

Chapter 28

Back in Time

━◦

I had the weirdest dream on Memorial Day 2009. I dreamed that I was starting over again, moving to Maryland after separating from my husband. It was so real, and yet I think it had to do with God trying to show me something I may have missed all these years.

In the dream, I was talking with my dad and he was telling me that I could live in his house. I was right back on Summer Hill again, sitting across from my dad and my stepmother. The strangest thing is that it was real—that is the way it happened when I got there, but as we all know that is not the way it stayed.

My relationship with my dad has always been strained, and I think that may be why I have had a problem with picking the wrong men. I think my mother and I have both done a pretty good job as single parents—certainly I grew into a successful businesswoman and my four kids are either in college or on their way there—but still sometimes it hurts me to not have a male figure and a two-parent home for my children. I love my children so very much and I work so hard to try to give them everything I did not have, but the biggest gift of all will be breaking the stronghold of single parenting.

Chapter 29

Britt

‎

It seems like my daughter Britt just grew up overnight. Britt was always a tomboy, always in sneakers. There was a time she couldn't walk in shoes; in fact, if you saw the movie *Love in Basketball* that was Britt, only instead of basketball her passion is track and field.

When we lived in Georgia I thought she and Tiff were so bad the principal must have my number on speed dial. Every week I was being called for the two of them fighting with someone, and if you saw them you would never believe it. They were no more than eighty pounds each, and both had long hair, pointy noses, and were light skinned. To look at them you would think they would be the stuck-up ones afraid to break a nail. It had gotten so bad I would meet them at the school bus just to make sure they didn't fight. The first words they would always say were "They bothered me first." Wow, these two little ones drove me crazy, and since I didn't fight much growing up I knew they'd inherited their dad's mean streak. The other girls would always bother them, which I think had a lot to do with jealousy because Tiff and Britt looked different. I now understand that they were just defending themselves, but my philosophy was to learn how to walk away. My two oldest will also tell you that I placed them on punishment for a whole year one time and wouldn't let them go outside because I was just tired of the fighting. Ms. Britt of course would sit by the window and try to get the kids to come to the door and ask if she could come out to play.

Britt was the comedian of the family. Her smile even looked funny for a while because she'd had a front tooth missing since she was one year old. One weekend she was visiting her dad's mother and fell in the bathtub and knocked her tooth right out. Of course she would be that way until her adult teeth came in.

We were watching home movies and came across one where Britt, always the comedian, decided to stuff toilet tissue in her sports bra and do a silly dance she made up for everyone. She got a little too close to my cousin Fufu and bumped up against her glasses. This little girl re-broke Fufu's glasses that were already taped up. She laughed so hard and said, "I broke her glasses with my titties!" After Tiff reminded her that I would see what she was doing on the video, she immediately ran in the room, took out the toilet tissue, and just started dancing by herself without the video camera.

If this little girl was at the table eating and didn't like something, she would slip it in her napkin and throw it away so you would think she ate all her dinner. And waking her up for school was always a headache. I would wake her up, leave the room, and later come back in and find her sleeping in the closet on the dirty clothes basket when she was supposed to be in the bathroom getting ready for school. There was one trip to the grocery store I'll never forget. Britt and Tiff were both looking out of the window. When the car stops that means the windows are going up, we are parked, and we are going into the store—at least that's what it means to normal little kids, but not my two nosey Ms. Know-It-Alls. They thought that meant stick your head out the window and see how close Mom is going to park to the curb. Well, on this particular day I wound up the window and opened the door and was about to close it and walk away. Unfortunately Ms. Britt failed to tell me I had closed Tiff's head in the window. Tiff was yelling, Brittney was laughing—it was a mess. Until this day they still talk about that.

All four of the kids have been very excited about being involved with this book and sharing their memories of our lives. Ms. Britt recently came clean about another incident that happened while we were still living in Georgia. Britt had a very bad habit of placing jewelry in her mouth, especially a necklace and a ring that had her name on it. One day I yelled at her "Don't put it in your mouth!" to try to keep her from sucking on that ring. Well, little Ms. Bad Girl at the time waited until I walked out the room and then she mocked me. She repeated what I said, "Don't put it in your mouth," and as she was mocking me the ring actually slipped down her throat. She started to choke. She was eating at the time, so I thought it was food she was choking over. I rushed over to give her the Heimlich maneuver and thank God I was successful—her throat was cleared but nothing came out of her mouth. I still thought she'd been choking on some food. Now I know that Britt had the ring in her mouth and while she was mocking me it accidentally went down her throat and she swallowed it. So I asked her, "Well, brilliant young lady, did you ever regurgitate the ring or did you pass your bowels and it came out?" Because she was so secret and sneaky she didn't know that it would come out of her bottom. Hopefully she flushed it down the toilet!

Because Britt was so light-skinned, when we lived in New York my uncle Tony used to call her "whitey." I didn't realize how that would affect her until one day after school she said, "Mommy, the little black girls and boys at school are bad." I asked, "Britt, what do you think you are?" and she said, "I'm white." I asked about the rest of us, and Britt informed me that she and J were white and the rest of us were brown. I immediately got on the phone and called my uncle and told him not to call her whitey anymore, because she thought it meant she was a white girl.

Sometimes you don't realize you have to be very careful of the words you speak; they may have a lasting effect on someone. The final straw that tore me and my dad apart was when he got angry with me because I would not pay to put hardwood floors in his house that we were renting from him. I finally said enough was enough, gave him my notice to move, and we moved out. Well, my dad, being the nasty person that he is, did not abide by the time for me to move even though the rent was paid all the way through the end of the month. He came in while we were in the middle of packing, and not alone; he had some guy looking at the house to try to act like we damaged it. Britt, who was fourteen at the time, just happened to pass by him and heard my dad saying to me, "Look at you. You think you are high up on your horse, but you are going to fall flat on your face." She then heard him lie to the man and say we damaged stuff and had the house nasty and dirty. Britt said, "Ma, why is he lying to that man? We didn't do what he's saying." I told Britt, "Don't worry, he's just a bitter man. Don't pay him any attention." Proverbs 18:21 Amplified states: "Death and life are in the power of the tongue, and they who indulge in it shall eat the fruit of it." When he spoke those words to me God blocked it, and what he meant to harm me turned out for my good. Again, how do you speak such words in a hateful way towards your own daughter?

What I didn't realize is this truly hurt Britt. She was only two years old when her dad left, and after I left my husband he didn't have anything to do with her and Tiff or even his own two children, Amber and J. Grandpa was Britt's father figure. After we moved, the kids saw him and my stepmother outside and spoke to them. Well, Grandpa just looked at them, rolled his eyes, and walked away without saying a word. As always my stepmother made an excuse and told them, "Babies, don't pay him any attention; he's just mad."

I didn't understand how deeply all this affected Britt until one day about three years later we were in church and there was an altar call. Bishop was standing in the gap for anyone that had been hurt and needed to forgive. He allowed the members to come up to the altar and call out the name of the person they needed to forgive so they could be set free. We had been attending the church for four years, and for the first time I saw Britt go to the altar. It turned out she had to forgive her grandfather. She could not understand how he would put us out in the streets, how he would tell his own child "you are going to fall flat on your face," but most of all she said, "We don't have a father [referring to her and Tiff since Anthony is gone]. He is our grandfather and I thought he would be there for us. Why wouldn't he be the male role model in our lives?" Britt was going through it so hard between the void her dad had left and the actions of her grandfather that Bishop asked all the mothers in the church to come around her and pray. Thank God that hold was broken off her life. God delivered her, and she was able to understand that none of what had happened had anything to do with her but that her grandpa needed to be helped.

Britt seemed to grow up overnight; she went from being a silly young girl to a responsible teenager. She stuck next to me like glue and stepped right in to help when Tiff was sick. Although we were scared that she was not responsible, especially when she got her license and car, she turned out to be just the opposite. With all her accomplishments and the medals and ribbons she has won, Britt at seventeen years old became the regional hurdle champion. I remember people teasing her and asking how she got over the hurdles with her height. LOL!

At seventeen years old, thanks to so many friends, The Meltzer Group, along with the bishops and the members of the church, Britt was able to raise enough money to represent the state of Maryland on the track and field team through Down Under Sports International. Britt and Tiff were also guests on Radio One and Praise 104.1 FM's *Matt Anderson Show*. Britt went to run in Sydney, Australia, for seven days and then went off to Hawaii for four days. She brought back four medals for the USA/MD team.

My daughter Tiff will be the first female in our family to graduate from college (none of the women, including myself, went past high school), and Britt is the first in our family, male or female, to actually get a passport and travel outside of the country. Generational curses are being broken! I am so proud of all four of my children and I love them so much. I will continue to be a role model and show them what my mom showed me: we can live without welfare. Unlike my dad, who with his jealous spirit never wanted me to do better than he had, I want my children to have far more than I could ever imagine. Britt is now in college running track and majoring in sports management. That former tomboy with the missing front tooth has grown into a lovely young lady now finding her own path in life—although she's still very much the comedian.

Two in college and two college bound. Glory and thank you to God!

Chapter 30

A Special Man, a Great Friend

—

Iron sharpeneth iron; so a man sharpeneth the countenance of his friend.
Proverbs 27:17

God, I have been waiting on you, following your lead. All I ask for is a straight man, a God-fearing man that can be my companion and be a positive figure for J and Amber. I've had so much disappointment with men. Every time I think it is too good to be true, it really does turn out that way. I believe that because I think very highly of this one special man and spoke about him to everyone God let Satan grab a hold of it. We have to safeguard things and not speak them into the air. We should keep some things to ourselves.

My friend is a man that I could talk with about God. I could give him a scripture and he would give me one. A man who knew when I needed encouragement, and I knew when he was tired from all of his work I could encourage him as well. We had such a connection towards one another. He was a ray of sunshine and he told me I was honeydew to him. A man who prayed for me without my asking, and I thanked God and prayed for him every night. A man that I could be myself with. I didn't have to be hard or strong when speaking with him; with him, I could be vulnerable. A man that I trusted wouldn't do me wrong; because of his position and stand for God, I always said he wouldn't let anything jeopardize his relationship with God. A man that would let me hear the music he was working on and I could tell him how awesome it was. A man that introduced me to a style of music I never thought I'd like and created a CD so great it made me fall in love with the style and listen to it every night. I could go on and on for days about everything good about him. I felt he was a seasonal angel sent by God. I spoke about him every chance I got to whoever would listen, and I think he did the same because he would call or send me texts when I least expected it.

The two of us could compliment and tell one another how we appreciated the other, as well as pray for one another. All I can say is I am guessing this was not the season and he is not the man God has for me. I know God will work things out for my good. I truly enjoy every conversation we have. I started to open up and feel very comfortable. He told me he felt a connection to me and it was a likewise feeling. I would speak to him for hours on the telephone and talk about anything with him. I think God used him to show me that companionship is a good thing, that love and affection exists. He did give me that feeling. I think he is such a wonderful man of God, and that made me trust him and feel comfortable with him. I felt like he wouldn't do anything to hurt me. I guess God had to grab my attention and let me know this man is human. I felt as though I was in a time capsule or inside the movie *Sleepless in Seattle*. I always wanted to feel an instant connection to someone; I always wondered how you know it's love right away. I saw those eHarmony commercials, and every time I was in contact with him I felt that. I adored him for the conversations we held, and I felt such a closeness and comfort with him without ever physically meeting him. I am grateful for that; he breathed life back into me. I glowed when I spoke with him and I glowed when I thought of him. I glowed so much thinking about him that at one appearance I had a twenty-five-year-old following me around the entire night. He saw something on me but didn't realize it was not me he was following but the God all over me.

I'm sure it wasn't easy for him to let me get away from him either. I for one know how good of a woman I could be. The entire time we spoke he always told me he was not in a relationship with anyone, didn't have a girlfriend; of course what he considers a relationship and what I consider a relationship are two entirely different things. He told me he had female friends. Well, although he still stands by his words of not being in a relationship, I knew it would only be right to back off. Through all of it, I got down on my knees and prayed for him, but as a woman of God I stepped away. I told him maybe we will catch one another down the road in different seasons of our lives, and if there is no one else connected to us that may get hurt, then and only then something may evolve between us. I am not selfish. I knew that if we went forward now it would not be blessed or covered by God. I continued and I thanked God for him being in my life. I value keeping him as a friend rather than being out of the will of God; it messes things up and no room would be left for friendship. This is my prayer:

"Lord, when can I be blessed with the husband you have for me? I am sitting here very sad, God, but grateful over the many months you allowed me to have fellowship through conversation with a man of God.

"I know people come into our lives for seasons and to fulfill your plan and purpose, but I really hoped, God, that we were going to have just all the time in the world to get to grow with each other. You know he made me laugh, and I can't figure out why I am so sad right now and feeling like I lost a piece of me. I know you give me discernment and when things do not feel right then I should go with my gut. God, when he told me that he was praying for me and that he thanked God for me it melted my insides. I haven't been interested in anyone for a long time, God, and I'm noticing I shut myself down completely. But you allowed him to bring me back to life. I even took back my life from my dad."

I learned a lot from him and from our fellowship. When you read this chapter, just know that you have a special place in my heart, you have a friend for life. I am grateful to you for raising the standards and showing me what kind of man I deserve out of a relationship, and I would have been by your side to the end—you know how they say, "that ride-or-die chick" (smiles). It's just that at the moment there was too much confusion going on and if God is in it there wouldn't be confusion. I thank you for being my encourager, my really good friend, and my confidant. I will continue to thank God every day. I pray for you every morning when I wake and every night when I lie down because I know you to be a man with a good heart.

I really miss talking to you, which we can't do as often now because of our schedules. Sometimes we would talk to nearly 3 a.m., often until one of us fell asleep, which was also you first, old man. But still, I knew backing away would be the right thing to do. My first priority was to show my daughters they never have to settle for any man and they definitely don't have to share one. We didn't because neither one of us would let it go that far and take us out of the will of God, but I wanted to teach them fooling around with a man will lead to nothing but trouble and you can be sure that what he does with you he will eventually do to you. So do not involve yourself in a relationship that starts off being unpleasing to God. I will remain single by choice because I chose God. He hasn't forgotten me, and I will wait until he blesses me with a godly man made in his image. Right now I have found a friend for life; however, I know that one day I will find my Adam from whose rib I was formed (Genesis 2:22). The following saying appears in different languages, all with the same meaning:

(English)
If you love something let it go; if it comes back to you it's yours, if it doesn't it wasn't meant to be.

(French)
Si vous aimez quelque chose de le laisser aller s'il vous revient de son exemplaire si elle doesnt it wasnt destiné à être.

(Spanish)
Si amas algo déjalo ir, si vuelve a ti la tuya si doesnt it wasnt destinado a ser.

(German)
Wenn Sie etwas lieben, lassen Sie es gehen, wenn es darum geht, mit Ihnen die verkaufen, wenn sie doesnt it wasnt sein soll.

Chapter 31

Always Seek God

Sometimes you receive the exact message you need at precisely the right time, and for that I have to say, "Thank you, Lord." I will stay in faith for God's favor and grace over my life. This particular night, I was sitting on the sofa after eleven o'clock watching the man of God Joel Osteen on television. The sermon was "Being Pruned to Blossom." I encourage everyone who reads this chapter to purchase a copy of the sermon; you will be blessed.

I have gone back and forth over whether or not I would write this chapter. I decided on my own not to write it and thought I should finalize the book. However, it was not sitting right on my heart; my spirit was so stirred up I felt like I had knots in my stomach. I spoke with my best friend Cheryl, and after I told her how I was feeling she said, "You have to write and tell people what happened because there are so many people out there going through the same thing." After speaking with her, I knew it was not about what I wanted but what needed to be heard.

I was feeling nervous about where I would end up. On that day, October 6, 2009, I made one of the hardest decisions I've had to make in a very long time. I decided to write and send a letter to withdraw my membership from the church I attended. I must say I have heard on many occasions and have seen people walk up to the altar seeking prayer because they were previously hurt by a church. I had been attending this church since 2005, and during that time I had so much spiritually sown into me by the mother and father of the house, I was always anticipating and couldn't wait until Sunday came. I knew on Sunday I would be refreshed by the spirit to take on the next week.

When the kids and I first attended the church, I was feeling lost, with nowhere to turn. This was after all that mess with my father between 2004/2005. I knew I needed a new foundation to build on, for both myself and the kids. Luckily for us, it turned out the church was near my house. As parents we pride ourselves in taking our children to church to begin the proper spiritual foundation needed in their lives; however—listen to me carefully—this time, at my weakest and at a very dark point, my children had the opportunity of taking me back to church and reigniting my love for the Lord. The youth pastors invited my kids to Sunday service after meeting them while doing an outreach program at the high school. Because of my children I was back in a place of peace, right where I was yearning to be. After attending once, I rededicated my life back to Christ and we never left; we liked it so much we attended regularly until I eventually joined the church. It became like a family to us. I sat on the second row behind the ministers, and from the time I got out of the car and walked towards the church people would say hi to me and call my name. I knew a lot of people in the church and they knew me. The two bishops were so inspirational to me as a parent and as the future wife I would be to whomever God saw fit to send me. I became close friends with their son the pastor and his wife. Never in a million years would I have believed it would come to this and I would have to leave my church home.

Church is often given a bad rap, but you should understand that the church itself doesn't hurt anyone; it's the people in the church who hurt one another, and worst of all, it's often the saints who hurt people. If such hurt came from another church member, so be it; I could take whatever comes. But what do you do when the pastor in whom you've confided your biggest secrets proves through his own actions that you can no longer trust him? When he betrays you and everything you told him becomes open game for anyone to know about you? I learned the hardest way not to put my trust in man; they are only human, and no matter what position they hold they can hurt you.

I need to say that as a woman and definitely a single parent I knew I needed to have God in my life; I needed the fellowship that whatever storm I was in brought peace. There is a lot that I can say but I will not go into great detail, not because of him personally but out of respect for the church and his parents that worked so hard through blood, sweat, and tears to build up the church. I realized that if you give a person control and authority if they are not ready for it, all of the worldly chaos will break loose; in this case, unfortunately, the place was throughout the house of the Lord. Power will be misused and abused, and in the end the church always suffers. I forgave my pastor; he has been consumed by worldly things and is operating outside of the will of God. He has a spirit over him that it is all about him: "What can you do for me? I should have this ... I deserve that ..." He wanted to be famous. His actions belong not in the body of Christ but in the entertainment industry, and he is willing to jeopardize the souls of church members, and worst, the church body itself, by exploiting the church and letting anyone that can help him get to his next level of worldly things gain access over the trust that the membership placed in him.

Be careful and limit the business you do with your pastor outside of church. I will not say all pastors, but definitely the ones that are "playing church." In my case he became so comfortable with me that it made me very uncomfortable. He said things around me, let me see him do things that hurt me to know about. A couple of times it hurt me to have to tell him, "Pastor, you are out of line, you are overstepping your boundaries, and you have no right to say or do some of the things you do." I respected my bishops to the highest authority, and many times I heard him being so disrespectful towards the bishops when talking to other people; he took on an "I'm in charge; if I say do it, it gets done" attitude; it was an attitude of "I run this church; they do what I say." I won't go into great details because there is so much that he has personally done which could have affected my way of thinking about a church, but because I had God in my life I didn't stray. What he should have realized was that anyone that has to pump himself up becomes less respected. The very same worldly people he spoke to came right to me and told me to steer clear from him, that he was just trying to use me to get what he could get and he thought it was all about him. You know why they were able to do that? Because people with game know when another is trying to run a game. They started to show their true colors, exposing one another, leaving each other out on a limb. When he knew I was fed up with his actions, he tried to write me a letter, but anyone who reads the letter can tell it was so out of God's will and that he was operating under a "cover my butt" system so that he could tell people he tried, that he reached out to me. I pray that he goes back and reads it, or even more so, lets his parents read it, and he will understand why I didn't respond to him. The one statement I clung onto was when he said that he has "personally done so much" for me. Wow—I confided in you as my pastor and when you gave advice or were there for me you turn around and talk about "all you've done" for me.

Again, there is a lot that I can say. I am only going to briefly give you a couple of things that truly hurt my heart.

I always tried to use the benefits of my job to donate back to the church. For over two years I paid for the church worship guides, the programs handed out in the church. I was very happy to take that load off the church so they could use funds to place into community projects. Previously they'd been outsourcing to a company to print the guides, which was a hefty expense. In return for printing the guides, I had a business card–type ad on the back of the worship guide that said it was sponsored by my company. I also became very involved with the annual golf tournament that the church held, the proceeds of which went towards scholarships for the children in the church. My company became the title sponsor, which meant we donated $10,000.

I am only going to say not what was done in partnership with the church but what followed. Pastor came to me and told me to change the checks from being issued in the church's name to the company he started for his record business. I didn't think anything of it and it really didn't matter; his response was they were all one and the same. I did this for nearly a year. During all of the chaos breaking loose in the church, in the midst of the pastor's transitioning to having the reins passed down to him, the financial administrator was the first person to step away. The new administrator, who also happened to be the pastor's cousin, took over. A few months later Pastor came to me and said that his cousin was having a fit because my company was writing the checks payable to his company instead of to the church and the church was not receiving the money. He asked if we could write two checks each month, making half payable to his company and the other half payable to the church. This threw up a very big flag for us. It was presented as being all in the same account; we were under the impression that when we made the change per Pastor's request he had cleared it with the bishops and they were fully aware. Right at that time Jacob, Dennis and I decided we were not going to get involved, we were not going to sponsor the worship guides any longer. Pastor sat in the office with us and asked us if we would pay at least half and still be able to have the guides sponsored by the dealership. We told him with the turn in the economy it was not feasible nor was it a good business decision. The same gentleman he gossiped to me about called me to ask me why I was paying such a large amount of money for the worship guides when they printed their own guides in the church office on the new printer they purchased. Of course it was mentioned in church the amount of expense my company picked up. Pastor never told me the guides were being printed in the church—we were completely under the impression everything was still being outsourced—and he continued to receive the same amount from me without telling me it was now costing less to print the guides.

Once Pastor came to me and acted like he was just visiting me. I didn't mind; it was always a great surprise. But this time the conversation really bothered me. He told me he had furniture being delivered to his house and he was short with the money. He asked me if I would use my position and ask the owners to loan him the money and he would pay it back; this was nearly $2,000. I felt embarrassed to go to them to ask because it made me feel like churches have already been given a bad name, and so many people try to find reasons for saying that pastors are crooks. I was not going to mention it to them, one, because this was my employer he was asking me to get money from, and two, I knew that they would use this as a way of looking down on the church and trying to twist it by saying he's leading the congregation and the church doesn't have anything. I told him I didn't feel right asking them. My next thought was that I was sure the bishops would give it to him; why was he not asking them or even borrowing it from his sister? Although I could not understand what would make him have furniture delivered when he didn't have the money to pay for it, I ended up loaning him my next month's rent money because at that time I had it, and yes, he did bring it right back to me the following Monday. I'm sure his wife didn't know; she is so sweet and such a woman of God that she probably doesn't know how he's misusing his power as a pastor to get favors done.

There was an incident in which one of his relatives was involved with a married man that I had introduced my pastor to. According to the relative in question, she called me since they had all met at the dealership and tried to explain her side, saying this man had told her he wasn't married, that his wife had cheated on him and that she could ask me. Well, when she did I told her I didn't know anything about that situation and I did not want to get involved. Pastor called me and said he was not going to let her mess up his doing business with this guy, that it was her fault and it was not the first time she messed around with a married man. His exact words were that he hated her and he was going to kick her out of the church. I said, "Whoa, Pastor. What are you saying? Apparently she needs help." This was a single mother he was speaking about. I told him, "Pastor, you may need to talk with her. Kicking her out of the church is not right. In fact, I could care less about him; he knew he was married, but she goes to our church. We can't throw her out there like that." To sum it up, he did kick her out of the church and I didn't see her for months before I left. It broke my heart because I would see her dropping off the kids to school and didn't know what to say to her.

The gentleman involved was someone I got into a business disagreement with. I decided I would no longer do business with him nor was he allowed to come back to the dealership because he had caused a scene when he got into a cursing match in the middle of the dealership with Jacob, one of the owners. Well, he had brought some customers to the dealership, and the dealership paid him money for the referrals. He then got some of these customers to file a false complaint against me. Yes, the customers had a legitimate claim because one was promised an extra key and the other's tags had expired—all of which was being handled by Jacob. Clearly, they were aware they had never spoken with me about any of this; they'd only had conversations with Jacob and I was not a part of the transaction. But this gentleman had them write a letter of complaint and didn't have Jacob's name anywhere on it, only mine. I received a phone call from my pastor telling me the people that filed a false complaint called his personal cell phone to complain about me but that he would not hear anything they had to say. What hurt was Pastor then turned right around and asked me to continue doing business with this guy; he asked me not to stop the referral program through which the dealership paid him. I told him there was no way I would deal with this man again—not after the situation with the cheating, the situation with the arguing in the showroom and the false complaint he convinced his friends to file. I told Pastor, "This guy is out to hurt me and make me look bad; why would you want me to do it all over again?" I knew the real reason behind it was the gentleman told Pastor he could help him get his records out. Again this was clearly about his personal gain and not the safety of his church members.

It came to the point where the asking for favors was overwhelming; I went from feeling like Pastor and I were the best of friends and being excited to do things with the church to it being overbearing. The only difference was he now manipulated his position in the church and my respect for the house of God to use for his own personal gain. The church had helped me one semester with my daughter going to college, and I repaid the benevolence they loaned me within two weeks, but my willingness to want to do things eventually became "Look, I don't owe you anything. I know you helped my family, but enough with the asking for things."

I got into a lot of disagreements with the Car Dealership owners because they did what I wanted to do for the church; they didn't want to but did it because I was okay with it. In the last conversation I had with them about that, they said, "Don't let him use you. He's using you and taking advantage of you." Ironically in the end when I was gone from the dealership the pastor tried to get into bed with the owners. I haven't a clue how that relationship is going.

Another incident happened when I was receiving the First Ladies Award. I had given Pastor complimentary tickets for the bishops, his wife, and his sister and her husband. Well, his sister's husband came to me and purchased two tickets. I was thinking to myself, "Great, more people," not realizing the tickets were for them personally. I mentioned to the pastor that his brother-in-law had purchased the tickets, and he said, "Good, because I wouldn't give her nothing; she wasn't getting anything from me."

I eventually ended up inviting his sister to the unveiling of the Sojourner Truth statue and she was so appreciative; she was great company and we all had a blast. Well, later that day she asked me what made me decide to invite her. I couldn't tell her it was because of the prior event and what happened with the tickets. After we got home I was on my way to the store and because we all lived right next to one another I ran into Pastor in the street. I told him how much fun we had and how great it was. His response was "Whatcha take her for? Don't be doing anything for her." I was stunned and I told him that was not right, he shouldn't be saying that.

Another time, because of my connections with the local radio stations and their personalities, the worship leader called me and told me he was giving a free concert and asked if I could get a personality to come and emcee the concert. After getting a couple of personalities from different stations to agree to help me support the event, I was trying to reach my worship leader on the phone and couldn't, so I called my pastor. He promptly told me not to let anybody call me to ask for anything; if it's not him, say no. He told me he was cancelling the event. I felt horrible because I'd heard the excitement in my worship leader's voice when he called me. Pastor then turned around and told me he wanted his own radio show and asked if I could connect him with the right person.

I could go on and on, because like I said, the pastor became comfortable around me and would say anything, especially since he thought he controlled me. My pastor was driving company cars from the Car Dealership—yes, my company cars—free of payments. Might I make it clear that his lovely wife was completely against accepting the cars in the first place. He thought he could drive any luxury car he wanted, just like I did as the general manager of the dealership. Well, he started complaining to me and bringing to my attention things that were wrong with the cars, and kept insisting they weren't doing the right things to the cars. Of course after it all boiled down, the owners would not let him drive luxury cars, they gave him basic transportation. Then I lost my job because I would not let my integrity be compromised and the owners of the dealership didn't like me saying no; they were trying to get me to back them on a lot of things which turned out to not be right, and I refused to do so. I was not going to keep going along with what they were doing. After I was gone from the dealership I left my pastor a telephone message letting him know I was no longer at the dealership and that he and his wife should go elsewhere to buy a car and then return the two cars they were driving from the dealership. Pastor didn't call me until almost a week later, and the first thing out of his mouth was that he went and met with Jacob and his brother but they didn't say anything about me. Okay, sure, right—then I knew he might just as well have made a deal with the devil himself. Well, I told him I was moving out of Jacob's house, and Pastor told me he could talk to Jacob and tell him to lower the amount of rent I was paying and they would do whatever he says because they owe him. After I left he helped them sell four cars; really it was to clear a financial obligation he had incurred with them. I asked him, "So tell me, how does that make you feel?" and his response was "What do you mean?" I said, "You know everything that was going on and what happened to me and you complained about the cars, so why would you send your members there to purchase cars?"

I never heard back from him after this, not even to see if the kids and I needed help moving or had even found a place to live. His response was "Hey, they don't go to my church." It went right over his head that it doesn't matter—even if it were a person on the street, he took an oath with God. What he didn't know was that I started praying for his family right after I got off the phone. I made it evident by the tone in my voice that I was both hurt and angry, not because he was just trying to clear himself but because his wife I'm sure had no idea what he did and in putting someone else's family in harm's way he could just as well have had something happen to his family. I prayed and asked God to block it, and thank God for his wife and family being true followers of God, they were protected.

I have so much more I can say about things that could have truly driven me away from church itself forever; however, what I will strongly express is (not mentioning names because you know who you are), I've already forgiven you and prayed for you. Aside from what he has done to me, as a pastor he will have to answer to God and will be held accountable for the souls of people leaving the church, the people forced out of the church solely because of his fame complex. It does not give anyone pleasure to sit in a church service when, because of the untrust, they can no longer receive the message being preached. When that time comes, you will leave. I am writing this because I want people to know I have been hurt and I may have left the church building structure, but I never left the presence of God. I didn't go back out into the world and back to my old ways with partying and drinking—though that could have easily been done, especially since that is a crutch for so many of us. The first thing I hear people say is "I was hurt by my church, and I'm not going back to church because the people are hypocrites." This is exactly what Satan is waiting for. He lurks around just waiting for the chance to step in. Most people do not have a clue that when Satan sees what God has placed on your life he will use anything to stop it. You can only be betrayed by someone you trust, so he will attack those close to you, which is unfortunate for them, sometimes not even knowing why they are under attack. I hear people say they don't have to go to church, but the Bible says in Psalm 107:32, "Let them exalt Him also in the congregation of the people. And praise Him in the company of the elders." In other words, we should gather together in the house of the Lord.

Yes, I was devastated. I did not have a church home. I felt alone, I felt lost and vulnerable. Although I had forgiven the pastor and lifted him up in prayer, still I felt like I'd lost my security blanket, my covering. What I didn't realize is that I am always covered by the blood of Jesus. I am here to tell you even if you have to find a closet, or sit in your living room, even in the middle of the kitchen floor or inside of your car, talk to God every day. I continue to talk to him, I pray every morning and every night, I read my scriptures, I read my daily devotions, I watched pastors on television and streamed online like Joel Osteen, Joyce Meyers, Dr. Jamal Bryant, and I have often visited Spirit Of Faith Christian Center in Ellicott City with Pastors Drs. Mike and Dee Dee Freeman. I do not care who it is, never let anything or anyone cause you to run from God. Man will get out of the will of God, but only you can remove yourself from God's presence. Just as I have witnessed by some of the things that I heard directly from the pastor's mouth. He has been in the world for a long time, and it worsened when the reins were being passed down to him.

When I made the dreadful decision to withdraw my membership, I went so far as to do things by order. As I mentioned earlier in the chapter, I sent to the main office of the church a letter to withdraw my membership. The letter I wrote was not long; in keeping with the fact of being careful and just trying to stay in the will of God by keeping to the order of things, I kept it short and to the point. I knew it would not be of God to join another church without first being released from my current church. Sad to say, I never received a response from the church; however, a church member made it his business to pick up the phone just to call and tell me that for his birthday he had lunch with the pastor, and in the midst of his trying to gossip about me to this gentleman, Pastor said, "Have you heard from your girl? She wrote a long letter to the church to withdraw her membership." This was a gentleman that I have not spoken to for a while. I halted ties with just about everyone, trying not to get caught up in the middle of gossip. Certainly I felt he played two sides and would call just to get things stirred up and try to find out just as much information as he gave out. I was angry after hearing this. My first reaction was "It's none of your business. My letter is between the church and myself; Pastor had no right to tell you anything about it." Then I thanked him for telling me about this conversation because, while the pastor's comments represented yet another breach of trust, at least that gave me confirmation my letter was indeed received. I still have yet to receive a letter of release from the church. I'm in line with God that idle gossip and not sending my release letter will be two more things he will be held accountable to God for.

I know that there are so many of you that have lost confidence and left a church. All I am trying to say again is that people in the church, from the pastor on down, are all human; we all make mistakes. Do not let them take you out of the will of God. We have to forgive them the same way God has forgiven us. We have to pray for them. I sat at home and sought God; I didn't just run right out to join another church. I prayed for covering over the bishops of the church throughout everything they are fighting against. You see, you can detect the wool being pulled over your eyes, but you have to pray for your leaders; Satan has now pulled out the silk. Satan slipped into the sanctuary to create chaos through the bishops' own son not because he is stronger than they are but because they were distracted with a lot of other things that were going on. Havoc was released throughout the congregation. You had members leaving the church; you had founding members (elders) leaving the church. When I found out the church worship leader was moving on, I told Pastor I felt so bad and I knew he was taking it hard because they were cousins. His response was "We don't need him anyway. He couldn't take us to the level we were trying to go." Wow—it hurt me to hear those words. This is the very moment that you have to keep the leadership of your church in prayer, especially for the mother and father of the church. When their son took over, his judgment was so tainted that discernment was placed in the direction of benefiting himself while making decisions out of the will of God.

There will be people put in place to pray over you that are not straight themselves. All kind of spirits running wild throughout the church. You have to learn how to pray for yourself and not let just anybody pray over you. I prayed the bishops would get relief from illness and everything else Satan had them under attack with and that they would take back the church so that it could get back to being the house of God I loved. When it is in line with God, God can be in the midst of any situation, God can open his mouth and blow a wind of fresh air through the church and just as many people that left, he can bring them back multiplied. People can play church when church is in chaos, they can sit there undetected stirring up trouble, but when God steps in and says to the storm, "Peace. Be still," he will make all the ungodly spirits scatter. Be careful. You see, I was not going to just run right out and join another church. You have to know what you are attaching yourself to; the first new church you run to may not be the place that God has for you either.

I did not badmouth the pastor, and especially not the house of God. I am saying this again; it's in my spirit that just in case someone missed it the first time, if it went over their head, I have to say it again. It's not the church that does anything to you, it's the people in the church, the saints of the church. Until now I have yet to tell people what has happened, and all of this isn't even the half of it. I received many questions from so many of the members asking why I left so abruptly. So many have voiced their own opinions about the very same pastor … I didn't agree with them or engage in gossip, not because of the person but because I am afraid of God; I am afraid that everything I have sown into the fertile ground the bishops prepared before me would be unsown. It was his very own actions that made it clear to all of them. They all ended the conversation by saying they know he was the reason for my leaving. Sad to say, apparently I was not the first person he has done this to and until he gets things right with God, I will not be the last.

Last but not least, I cannot stress enough to women and men, you cannot use the church as a dating scene to find your husband or wife. There is this misconception that you will go to church and find a good man or a good woman. Yes, there may be a few diamonds in the rough, but most people do not go to church until they get into a crisis that only God can get them out of. Needless to say, that person you meet can be jacked up with some serious issues. Single parents trying to find a daddy for your kids, please be mindful of your kids around that person you meet in the church, the person you may sit next to, the person that may be trying to mentor your child, adding them to the many other children they try to mentor and hang around. Things may not always be as they appear. They will be more interested in your child than in you. Just remember that Satan was a fallen angel, he ministered through praise and worship as a choir member, and therefore he and his people can quote the Bible like there is no tomorrow. I found God when my life was a mess, and of course God does not mind; in fact, he shows us his glory and how he is the fixer of all things. People are getting delivered from all kinds of things in the church, even incest, child molestation, adultery, drugs, etc. But as a single parent, always place your kids' safety first. I know we have to leave things to God; however, if you go there for all the wrong reasons, you will be working outside of the will of God. Remember God protects babies and fools, but you have to pay attention when you feel something is just not right about a person, man or woman—that's God filling you with discernment.

There are wonderful, good people in the church; just remember Satan also places his pawns there to stir things up. In this time and season we are in, Satan is definitely attacking our children. You cannot put it on the church leaders; they cannot be everywhere, so we need to go into motion and protect our cubs. They will have a fictious lifestyle and have everyone thinking they are such a wonderful person. They will pretend to be interested in a mother/father when in fact they may be eyeing your children. You can see them out in public with a man/woman just for the purpose of being on the down low. They will tell you that their live-in lover of the same sex is a relative of some sort. I'm sorry to have to give it to you so raw and uncensored, but when it comes to my kids I don't care how good the church members may say someone is, I don't care if I sit next to them in church every Sunday, could care less if everyone thinks they are such a good person or thinks that you will make a perfect couple with that individual—believe me when I ask you to still be very cautious. What is done in darkness will always come to light; just don't let your child be drawn into something that may be unhealthy for them. Mentor them yourself if you have to.

And those who know Your name will put their trust in You; For You, Lord, have not forsaken those who seek You.
Psalm 9:10 NKJV

Chapter 32

God Is Good

~~~

We all know the saying "God may not come when you want him to, but he will be there right on time."

Remember a few chapters ago I said that 2009 was turning into a momentous year for me? Well, "momentous" can refer to both tremendous opportunity and difficult challenges. Now we're really getting to the challenging part. Eventually, after I'd worked there for two years, the Car Dealership and I had so many professional disagreements I refused to be moved and let my integrity be jeopardized so they decided to replace me. Suddenly I found myself unemployed in the middle of a recession. I applied for unemployment, but it turned out there was a big disagreement over whether I had actually quit or been let go. According to the Car Dealership, my job was still there if I wanted it. But did the unemployment office really think I would just quit a job in this economy, when dealerships were closing right and left? Well, it turned out they listened to the Car Dealership and denied my unemployment. Now I wouldn't even have temporary income to help me get through.

To make matters worse, at the time I was renting a townhome mortgaged by Jacob, one of the Car Dealership's owners. Back when I first moved in, we all thought it was such a great idea. The location was perfect: I wouldn't have to switch my kids' school, and it was close to work and to my church home. But that was before my relationship with the Car Dealership turned sour. I was served papers stating I was to appear in court because I was being sued for $2,400 plus legal fees for nonpayment of rent. I felt totally betrayed at that point. I had worked so hard for this company for two years, and my only repayment was to have my unemployment claim fought and to be sued over the rent. But still I trust God in all that happens in my life and I will tell his goodness every time I get a chance.

This was happening in September. Two months prior I had given them notice that I would be out by the end of August and not residing there in the month of September. The place was too expensive and Britt was getting ready to go to college, so I thought it was time to downsize to something smaller and more affordable. With the economy in a downturn and things being slow at the dealership, I was having trouble even paying the utilities at this place. I said I would give two months' notice so they could find a new tenant. They tried to offer to let me pay reduced rent of $1,800 and give me some extra money for other bills so I could stay there, but I really didn't want that. I told them no, I would prefer to find something I could afford on my own. Fortunately my receptionist Carissa overheard me telling them that I would rather downsize. If I couldn't afford it then maybe it was not of God for me to continue to be there. For a while if I was going through something I would pray for God to take care of it; however, as I've matured in Christ I realize God is in the midst of everything right from the beginning. He was telling me that was not the place for me to be.

So in August I went to look at a couple of places, trying to find something inexpensive. I was humbled and only looking for a roof over my kids' heads at this point. I found an apartment but was turned down when I applied for it. My first thought was *Where are we going to go? If the judge makes me pay $2,400 and I don't have any money, how are we even going to afford the next month's rent at the new place?* Finally I got us a place, but only with my mother's help because I was unemployed.

Still I had this court date hanging over my head. But God knows what's going to happen before it does. When we least know it, God has us covered. All we have to do is pray for him to give us wisdom. For the two months of July and August I had paid the $2,400 regular monthly amount, but that was through my two months' notice. Well, I prayed and I had my girlfriends in agreement with me. My BFF Cheryl prayed, "God, you know her finances and you know her situation. God, when Shanise goes into that courtroom I pray that she doesn't have to pay one cent." At the same time I was on my knees on the floor of my new place. I prayed, "God, I don't have the money to give them and still be able to pay rent here."

My old employee Carissa picked me up on the morning of my court date. I had to go to district court, and she said she wanted to go with me to be my witness. My case was next to the last to be called. Jacob had his representative handle the case; neither he nor his wife showed up to face me.

The judge said, "Ms. Craft, they are saying you owe them money for the month of September." My two months' notice was paid through the end of August. Now they didn't ask for the amount, they changed it back from $1,800 to $2,400. They also never mentioned that they asked me to stay on and instead of the lowered rent they wanted me to sign a new lease at the $2,400, which I refused to do.

I responded, "Ma'am, I gave them two months' notice that I would be moving out, so they knew I would not be living there in the month of September which they are now trying to sue me for. My rent was paid through August as we had previously agreed."

Well, the lady there handling the case for them didn't know anything, so the judge gave us a minute to step outside and work it out. When we went back before the judge Carissa was at the table with me; we had both been sworn in earlier because she was my witness. Jacob's representative first said that I had no right to give verbal notice and that I have a legal contract with them to give thirty days' written notice. I told her to show me that contract. She then asked the judge for an adjournment, which I objected to. Here they are suing me in court and now trying to get the case adjourned when I showed up prepared to proceed. The case wasn't even fair to begin with, and then the amount they were suing me for was unbelievable. After a couple of minutes of talking the judge finally said, "I agree with the defendant and I deny the adjournment. We will hear the case now." So I went to trial right there. After she'd heard both sides the judge said, "I rule in favor of the defendant. You do not have a case against her."

Guess what? God worked it out so I didn't have to pay one penny. It was just as the prayers were sent up. Glory to God! He showed me, Carissa, and everyone I testified to that he comes right on time. Now when I went to the unemployment office to appeal the denial of benefits, I would be able to show that not only was my job not there like they said it was, but they tried to evict me also. My prayers were going up to God that the outcome of the appeal would be in my favor. I have victory, I claim it in Jesus' name, and let no weapon formed against me prosper. Amen and amen.

God didn't just bless me once to tell about it; he blesses me again and again. He closed one door and opened another. I was able to move out before Satan had his chance to have me evicted and left homeless.

Chapter 33

Apartment Life

The realities of apartment life came as a big change for all of us. Ever since we moved from Georgia, the kids and I had lived in either a townhome or single-family home. But now since we had to move out of Jacob's townhome we'd gone from a four-bedroom four-bath house to a two-bedroom one-bathroom walkup apartment on the third floor. I was very grateful to God for having a roof over our heads. It certainly could have been worse; we could have been in a worse place or even homeless with the winter coming. We tried to make that first apartment feel like our home, but it just didn't.

I told you about all my earlier experiences with mice. Well, guess what? We didn't actually see Mickey Mouse in there, but I did find some droppings. I was in denial at first, thinking maybe we just tracked something in from the outside. I was never happy with the building we were in, but I was appreciative for whatever we had and decided to just suck it up and wait until God saw fit to move us. Well, after the maintenance people took four mice out of our apartment, I didn't feel so appreciative anymore; I walked right over to the leasing office and put in a transfer request to switch apartments. We could move to another building two streets over and directly across from the leasing office, but we'd have to wait two weeks. I just prayed for God to help us until then; this was going to be the longest two weeks of my life. I'd already decided that if we saw a mouse in the second apartment I would have to find somewhere else to live. That would be too bad, because the kids loved their schools and they had been outside more in the thirty days we'd lived in that apartment than in all the years we'd been in Maryland. They were definitely house kids before.

You know you have to watch what you speak into the air because Satan will try to get a hold of it and cash in on it. Everyone knows my fear of mice stems all the way back into my childhood and young adult life. So while writing this book I wrote about my fears and even spoke about them, and then I ended up in an apartment infested with mice. Well, guess what, Satan? You are a liar! Regardless of how it may have looked and how embarrassing it was, I was grateful that my kids and I had a roof over our heads, and I still trusted God. You see, I know this is not what God has for me, but if I have to walk through this because he wants me to face my fear, I definitely will stand on God's word for my life.

I was not going to get comfortable in that apartment because I was waiting on God to move us to our own house. I was also paying rent on a storage space each month because we could hardly fit anything into the apartment, just the necessities. In one bedroom I had two beds—Amber's full-size bed and J's twin-size bed with the drawers attached to the bottom. It was a very tight squeeze, but I needed the bed so that when Britt came from the college dorm on winter recess she could share the bed with Amber.

This experience humbled me, after years of living in townhouses where we really didn't hear anything from the neighbors and barely even saw them. One day Amber came into the apartment and said, "Ma, there is a lady having a fight with a dog."

I said, "What? How do you know that?"

She responded, "I can hear a lady screaming and a dog barking."

"Well," I said, "Amber, maybe the lady is in a fight with someone and the dog is barking."

Next thing I knew, I heard a bunch of kids and a lady yelling. Apparently the boyfriend or husband—we kept to ourselves, so who knew who he was?—was trying to leave and they were fighting because she didn't want him to. I was ready to call the police because I thought she needed help, but then I heard her say to him, "Just get your ass in here." They closed the door and I didn't hear anything else.

A couple of hours before all the commotion, I heard the fire department banging on the same neighbor's door. I guess she was sick. Well, I was waiting to see if they took her in the ambulance, but they made her walk down the stairs. I guess they said she was just a little over their weight limit, but they kept asking "Are you okay?" while making her walk—go figure. Her kids were going to be walking home with J soon after school, and I was going to ask this lady if she wanted to leave her keys for me to let them in, but then I had to remember that not everyone is kind. I didn't want her to think I was in their business. I already knew they were yelling and fighting. Surely this wasn't the first time and will not be the last. Everyone else in the building seemed very quiet and kept to themselves.

Sadly, it happened again—the police kicked in the door to the apartment next door to me. The kids and I were watching TV and I heard a little girl in the hall saying "I'm scared, I'm scared." Her mother called her name and told her to get back in the house. I then heard the mother asking the man what he was going to do with the vacuum cleaner. Then their door closed and I didn't hear anything else. Once the mother had gone back into the apartment I thought the little girl was inside. Well, apparently the little kid (who couldn't be any more than eleven years old) had run upstairs to the neighbor's apartment above mine and that neighbor called the police. I heard banging on the door and it was the police breaking the door down. They handcuffed the man; I'm sure he resisted because he looked a little banged up in the hall. One out of the five police officers took the mother upstairs to get her daughter. Meanwhile, the other two children were still inside the apartment crying. After I realized all the events that took place I was so disgusted that the mother did not go after her daughter. When the paramedic asked the child if that was her father she said no, it was her stepdad. I hope that since he was arrested the mother keeps him out now. I'd already heard two arguments from them in just four weeks. I'm sure this was a regular routine for them. I pray that those children are taken in by someone in that family who is responsible enough to care for them. I would hate to see that something happened to them.

I have never been more humbled in my life and cannot wait until God blesses us with our own home, a quiet safe haven.

I had a meeting with a couple of my friends about future plans. When the meeting was over one of them reached into their pockets and gave me some money. They said, "Use this and get you and the kids some food." You see, they had once been out of work in a situation similar to mine. They knew how it was to not have anyone. Everyone is your friend when you are in the limelight, but the minute your situation changes you do not see those same people. In the midst of crisis is where you will find your true friends. I didn't want to take the money because I know we are all transitioning into other positions and they could have used it themselves, but I had to take it. They were trying to be a blessing to me, and I didn't want to refuse it and block their blessing from God. God knows I needed it and I appreciated it so much.

If you stay in faith, just believe God because God is so good. It ended up taking a little more than two weeks for the leasing office to move us to a new apartment, but to God be the glory, because we were switched from a two-bedroom to a three-bedroom. The larger apartment would have been $250 a month more, but because of the experience we had with the neighbors' cleanliness, management upgraded us without increasing the rent. Thank you, Jesus. Now Britt will have her own room when she has to leave college campus for school breaks. The apartment is set up roommate style so she actually has the peace of being on the other side of the apartment alone for even more privacy.

To try to leave this chapter on a lighter note, I must say that my kids love their new schools, their new friends. Well, we all know kids say the darnedest things. My ten-year-old son Jesurun came home from school one day and said the lunch lady asked him if he wanted a leg, a thigh, or a breast. He asked her what was the difference, and as he stood there trying to figure it out she interrupted his thought and said the breast is the white meat, and the rest is dark meat. He then asked her why can't he have tan chicken; he wanted it mixed. So now he thinks white girls have big breasts and black girls have big thighs and legs. He wants a mixed girlfriend so that he could have all of it. Then of course Tiff, Britt, and Amber wore him out laughing about it, and he said laughing he didn't want dark meat, dark meat is crazy!

Chapter 34

National Congress of Black Women Awards

⁓

The way God works is amazing. Our lives are already planned and mapped out, just waiting for us to reach each particular moment in time. Remember it is not when we want it, it's when God wants it. It's not if we think we should be a part of something, it's if God lets us be a part of something.

I had to say those words because I need you to understand the greatness of God. In the fall of 2009, I was headed into another difficult time. Before me were trials that would humble me and break me down, but it was through those trials that God would set my feet on a new path, a path that would lead me to new life.

A couple of months back I volunteered to answer the telephone on the St. Jude's Radiothon being hosted by Cathy Hughes' Radio One and St. Jude's Hospital. I was sitting in the room with some amazing people. We just were all pumped up and ready to help raise money, especially on our watch. That particular day our Radio One location in the state of Maryland helped raise one hundred and twenty thousand dollars. That money would go directly to research and hospital care. While I was at the radio station all heck was breaking loose at the Car Dealership (this was while I still worked there).

A few months earlier I was nominated to receive an award from the National Congress of Black Women. I was nominated in the business category because I was the first female African American GM of a luxury car dealership in Maryland, and much to my surprise I actually won the award for Business and Philanthropy. The awards ceremony was scheduled for September 27, 2009. Now this was in the midst of further heck breaking loose in my life—namely, losing both my job and my home.

My point right now is that you should never try to figure out what God has for you. You see, I started feeling really bad about that award. I started second-guessing and feeling it just wasn't right for me to get it. But you know where that doubt was coming from? That was Satan trying to get into my head. I felt that I was taking up someone else's spot, that I was standing in the way of the person that award was truly meant for. How could I deserve such an award, such an honor, when my life was such a mess? But I'll tell you this: On the day of that awards luncheon and all through the entire month, God had me right where he wanted me.

The other honorees were: Kimberly Anyadike of California, the first African American teen to become a transcontinental pilot; Lavern Chatman, president and CEO of the Northern Virginia Urban League; Janet Langhart Cohen of Maryland, author of *Anne and Emmett;* Regina Kelly from Texas, the subject of *American Violet;* the Honorable Marcia Fudge, Democratic Congresswoman from Ohio; Judge Denise Langford Morris of Michigan, the first black circuit court judge in Oakland County; and Peter Harvey, former federal prosecutor and the first African American to serve as attorney general of New Jersey, who on this day received the "Good Brother Award" for domestic violence work.

Allison Seymour, anchor for Fox 5 DC, was the hostess and emcee for the event, along with Michelene Bowman as the announcer. There were so many people in attendance, but the person that most grabbed my attention was sitting right next to me at the table: Congresswoman Sheila Jackson Lee. I remember her looking directly at me and encouraging me to continue as I accepted the award and gave my acceptance speech. It was amazing and so awesome.

I told them how appreciative I was to receive this honor and to be part of such a prestigious organization. When I was a child I had no idea such an organization existed, but I wish we'd been privileged to know about the National Congress of Black Women and the wonderful things they contribute to young women, particular young women of color. I went on to say, "I am a single mother and now I have an organization to share with my children. I have a daughter that will be graduating this year from college in business management, and I have another daughter that just returned from Australia and Hawaii running track and representing the United States of America. I can see the generation of my children far exceeding all that I have done." That was just a small portion of what I said, and through it all I had the congresswoman's complete eye contact and she nodded, showing she was very pleased to hear what I had to say.

I told them that the women I looked up to when I was growing up were my mother and my aunts. No, they weren't in the best financial situation, but they never moped around and never let money get the best of them. My times around all of them would be spent laughing and joking. And the men in my life … my grandfather did not go past the third grade; he had to drop out of school and go to work to help take care of his family. My grandfather did not know how to read or write, but he never let us grandkids know it. If I brought a project home from school and showed it to Pops, he would sit there as though he was reading it right along with me with a proud smile that would light up any dark room.

Outside of my family, I watched television and found more female role models. I would watch Oprah and daydream all the time about being on the *Oprah* show, sitting next to her doing an interview. Oprah is a woman I am so inspired and fascinated by. When I watch the things she does, helping millions of people and making dreams come true, I pray for her to be covered and continuously blessed. I say it carefully because we can never say "I want to have what she has" because she has openly told her story. Although I have not endured the things she has openly spoken of regarding her life, I know that if she could take what she has experienced and turn into the empire she has, then I can take where I have walked through and use it to reach millions of people as well in hopes of playing a role in someone's life, changing their path and steering them clear of destruction. Two other women I watched were Whoopi Goldberg (I remember hearing years ago that she once was on welfare; reading it I didn't know how true it actually was, but I knew right there I was encouraged that I didn't have to be a statistic), and Cicely Tyson (I watched her pave the way for so many African American actresses). I watched women who would stand up for what they believe and who walked through many fires in their childhood and became very successful. I knew by watching them that I could do whatever I wanted. I knew by watching my grandfather that I would not let the fact that I became a mother at eighteen and never walked across the stage at my high school graduation hold me back. I would not let my circumstances be a crutch. I was not going to go on welfare; I was going to be very successful. My lifelong dream was to go on *The Oprah Winfrey Show* and meet her. I have spoken that into the atmosphere so much that I made believers out of my family and now I have my family saying, "Girl, you are going to be on *Oprah*."

After the ceremony I had a woman come up to me and ask me to do a book signing at her organization. At that moment again someone was telling me they wanted to hear more of my testimony. However, I didn't have a book … yet.

Chapter 35

Hospital Emergency Room

One night in the fall I had to take Jesurun to the emergency room. I'd been sick for about a week, and unfortunately after I got semi-better J ended up getting sick. I always have to watch him very closely; he gets sick every fall with the change of the weather. He might only get sick once or twice a year, but once he does it's very hard to get him well again. J had been down for over a week this time, and with him having bronchitis I watched him very closely at night to ensure his breathing was okay. Well, that went on for four days before I decided to take him to the hospital. During the day he was just fine playing video games, dancing to music on his iPod—normal things—but at night he started to get a fever all over again. I took him to the emergency room because it was eleven in the evening. We got there, and the minute I walked in I immediately felt those knots forming in my stomach. All you could see was employees and patients in white masks because of this swine flu epidemic. They wanted me to put a mask on J when I checked him in him, but I couldn't because his nose was stuffy and the mask would cover his mouth. The clerk told me to find a place by ourselves to sit. Amber, J, and I didn't get back home until 4:30 a.m.

The doctor kept us there to perform an x-ray on J's chest. She said that since his ears, throat, and nose were clear he may have fluid in his lungs. I walked over with him to get the x-ray, but the minute the doctor told me what she was doing I started praying. You see, I didn't want to wait to hear what was wrong. I started to intercede to change the outcome. I prayed that God would send his angels into the x-ray room before him and clear any lingering spirits. I prayed that this was a child of God and Satan has no authority over him because through his stripes he will be healed. I said, "God, I know your will is going to be done, not ours, but please cover the x-ray and tell me how to deal with any negative result." J was in the best of spirits. Amber wanted to lie on the hospital bed, so she was snoring while J sat on my lap listening and playing with his iPod. We waited for about an hour and a half, and thank God the test came back normal. No pneumonia.

I asked the doctor if she was going to give him anything to clear his chest since she thought he had fluid on his lungs. She said her son had the same symptoms—he was okay during the day but had a fever at night. She said it could go on like that when it's viral, and since today was Friday we should wait until Monday to follow up if the fever persisted. I always make sure the kids have coats on when they go outside, but the doctor said that has nothing to do with it.

Thank you again, God, for revealing yourself to me in the time I cry out for you.

Chapter 36

Losing Flash

Not only did we lose some privacy and pride when we moved to the apartment, we lost our beloved pets. Our two goldfish did not survive the move. They were about thirteen years old; Britt and Tiff had won them in a county fair up in New York when we still lived there. And then, a few weeks after we'd been in the complex, we had to give our pet dog away. Flash had been with us for two years, ever since he was just six weeks old. He just could not get used to the apartment. We weren't even supposed to bring him with us because I would have had to pay an additional $500 deposit and a monthly pet rent fee. Besides that, apartment living was too chaotic for him; it was not the same as the quiet house that he was accustomed to.

We smuggled Flash in because our first apartment was in the back of the complex. This worked for about a month. Flash would bark all the time, but the neighbors didn't care. The maintenance guys were also very cool and didn't say anything when they came into the apartment and saw him. The problem was those mice. Because of the mouse infestation, we had to move to a building two streets over near the leasing office. There was no way we could get away with keeping Flash there; someone in the office was sure to see us with him. Besides, it was not fair to Flash to keep him there. He was a nervous wreck, barking all the time at the different noises, even the sound of cars outside. We knew when we moved in there that he could not come with us, but it was so hard for us to part with him we couldn't let him go. My biggest concern was the kids walking him early in the morning before school and late at night. There were just too many people around the complex, and I didn't trust the children being out there with Flash.

So many people inquired about Flash when I placed the ad. I pulled the first ad because it was too hard to let him go. The second ad brought in quite a few couples who were looking to add to their family. I received an e-mail from Dana saying she fell in love with my dog and would love to meet him. I had several conversations with this couple through e-mail and on the cell phone. They had a big yard and were looking for a puppy for their four-year-old daughter. Ironically, before they moved to a house they lived in the same complex I'd just moved to. The husband, Mel, came over to spend some time with Flash. Flash barked at first like he would always do, and then he warmed up to him. Brittney, Amber, and Jesurun were there. Mel thought maybe he should have come when the kids were not home, but I told him it was perfect that they could meet him and we could all see how Flash would be in good hands. He told the kids they could visit and even call to see how Flash was doing. That sealed my decision to give Flash to his family. When Mel told me that when I returned his phone call he had just gotten off the phone with his pastor, I was comfortable that they would love Flash just as much as we did.

My oldest, Tiffanie, couldn't come over to say goodbye. She called my mother in New York crying. Britt was crying. Amber didn't even want to walk out with Flash. J was sick so he couldn't go out. Britt and I walked Flash down to the car, and he jumped in without any problem. I guess he thought he was going for a car ride with us. I tried to resist calling to check on Flash right after they left. Brittney said, "Mom, don't call him yet. Let them be with him." The kids didn't know that I did send them an e-mail that day and followed up the next day just to make sure Flash was okay. It broke my heart to have to give Flash up, and I shed quite a few tears over it. I prayed that his new family would give him a safe, loving home and a nice place to run and play. I miss you, Flash.

As much as I hated to see Flash go, I did feel better knowing that the kids wouldn't have to be outside alone anymore. Until God saw fit to bless us with our own home, I planned to always be there and never leave J and Amber in the apartment alone. Once everyone was inside we wouldn't have to worry about going back out. I didn't feel the neighborhood was bad; in fact, I spoke with a few people who all said it was a good area, and even Mel said they didn't have any problems here but they moved into a house when their daughter came along. Things happen though, and I just really didn't feel comfortable with neighbors and guests and the kids having to walk Flash.

I keep in contact with the family and recently spoke with Mel and his wife. They love Flash, and he is doing very well with an energetic four-year-old to keep him company.

Chapter 37

Sleepwalkers

⁓

Britt came home because J asked her to. She called me and said she wanted to cry because J missed her and wanted her to leave campus because he was sick. So I went to pick her up. Now Britt sticks to her workouts regardless of whether she is at school or at home. She always runs her miles and goes to lift her weights. One day Amber decided to go up to the gym in the apartment complex for a workout with Britt. Needless to say, that didn't last very long. They were back after only an hour. Amber said she will never go with Britt again because Britt did not show her any pity.

Amby went into the room, J and I were on the sofa, and Britt decided to take the loveseat. She fell asleep, and after about an hour J was asking how long she was knocked out so that he could wake her up. I told him to leave her because she is up at five o'clock every morning and is running by six.

Some more time passed, and then all of a sudden Britt jumped up and ran to the door saying, "J is still outside. I have to get J." I said, "Britt, Jesurun is right here. You are dreaming. Now come and sit back down." My child was sleepwalking. Britt's normal habit was to talk in her sleep every now and again, but this time was scary. I asked her if she had done that at the dorm, and she said no. One time she got up to look for her telephone because she thought she was late for class and her roommate told her it was ten at night.

When this happened it rekindled a memory from when I was around eight or nine years old. I called New York and spoke with my mother and Uncle Tony to see if they remembered exactly how old I was. My mom laughed and said, "I was wondering if you were going to put that in the book." She yelled out to my uncle to ask how old I was, and he confirmed that I'd been eight going on nine years old. My mom recalled the story for me.

Everyone was asleep and Mom heard the door unlock and open. She said she and Jack, her old man, rushed to get up and get to the door. By the time they went down the hallway Mrs. Erma, the neighbor from the apartment in the front, was walking back to tell my mom I was okay and I was in her apartment. Apparently I left my room, unlocked the door, and went down the apartment building hallway. Still asleep, I knocked on Mrs. Erma's door. When she saw it was me she let me in, but I didn't speak to her. I walked in and just sat on her sofa like I was waiting to watch the television.

After that incident my mom got so scared she put a chain lock and a double lock on the front door to try to keep me from running out. She thought I had gone into the street, and her heart was racing until she saw Mrs. Erma. She spoke with the doctor about what happened, and he told her that I had a nervous condition and my mind was always gathering things even when I was asleep. I was just nervous that I would miss something going on around me.

Thank you, God, for your covering.

Chapter 38

My Morning's Daily Inspiration

⌒

Knowing that God can use all things for good is more than enough reason to give thanks in everything. Giving thanks in difficult circumstances is a small detail that makes a big difference.
—Julie Ackerman

Money got so tight I had to call the Energy Assistance Program. I never wanted to get to this point. Although I have always been obedient to God, I put my trust in man. God has never failed me, but man has done it every time. I could be bitter about my experience with the Car Dealership. That was the lowest-paying job I ever had in the car business, and the minute I put my foot down and would no longer go along with some of their practices, the first card they pulled was replacing me with someone and then the second card was trying to evict me out of Jacob's house. I had to go to court because Jacob tried to sue me, including an eviction; however, on the record the district court judge ruled in my favor.

I prayed to God each and every day that I needed to get out of the situation there, and he helped me—he shut the door, he closed that chapter in my life, and I was grateful. I was at peace with myself and God.

You must understand that I was grateful even though I didn't have any money and had every bill due, I had my daughter in college calling for groceries, I had my ex-husband trying to pay even lower child support even though I am only collecting for one child, I left my church home of nearly five years, I had my mother's bills due because she tried to help me by giving me her bill money. My best friends barely had money for gas, I was feeling under the weather with a sore throat, and the guy who said he would buy my dining room set never showed up to get it (I thank God for that— he knew my heart was humble, but maybe he was protecting me from something else). I was under attack every day, but I continued to trust God, and I believed that everything God was allowing me to go through was because he had a bigger purpose for me. I thank you, Jesus. Satan cannot do anything God would not allow, so I won't give him credit anymore for anything.

Just like the other morning when I got a flat tire, my normal quick response would be "the devil is a liar," but I caught myself and I shouted, "Thank you, Jesus!" You see, that flat tire could have saved me from a blowout. It could have been far worse, but God shut that car down. Glory and praise to God! I love you, Father, and I thank you for seeing fit to use a single mother of four children straight out of Washington Heights off of Sugar Hill, New York.

My situation looked impossible. Turning it around was beyond me. The list of "could nots" was long: I could not open my own dealership, could not restore and give myself an 800 credit rating, could not buy a house of my own, could not become a multimillionaire by my fortieth birthday like I told myself I would, could not break clear of the Car Dealership and have them leave me alone, could not find a decent and equally yoked man, could not buy my own jet and deliver my testimony to people all over the nations, could not heal the illnesses my family and I faced. BUT thank you, Lord, because through Christ Jesus all things are possible. Nothing is impossible. God can send me someone to just hand me a check for money to fund the dealership, God can and will restore my credit, God can put me in my very own house, God can instantly make me a multimillionaire, God can take care of the Car Dealership, God can send me a strong, six-foot-two Godly man, one that I can be in the word with so that we could worship together and raise our family, and God can heal in accordance to his word.

But He was wounded for our transgressions,
He was bruised for our iniquities;
The chastisement for our peace was upon Him,
And by His stripes we are healed.
Isaiah 53:5

You see, I decided to write down what I was asking for, write down the impossible for me, because when God blesses me, when I have all those things that I speak into existence, I want there to be no mistake that it was because of my father in Heaven. All glory, honor, and praise will I give him, and I will continuously speak his praises. What I can do with his grace is tell my story all over the world. Let people know he is God and through him nothing is impossible. I know I am writing this to tell everyone about God's grace and favor, but thank you, Jesus. I have to get up and dance right now.

And the Lord answered me and said, Write the vision and engrave it so plainly upon tablets that everyone who passes may [be able to] read [it easily and quickly] as he hastens by.
Habakkuk 2:2

For the vision is yet for an appointed time and it hastens to the end [fulfillment]; it will not deceive or disappoint. Though it tarry, wait [earnestly] for it, because it will surely come; it will not be behindhand on its appointed day.
Habakkuk 2:3

Father, thank you that in every trial, challenge, and difficulty, you are behind the scenes working things out for our good. Help us to see your hand in everything. Amen.

Chapter 39

"I Get It"

～

A good man leaves an inheritance to his children's children.
Proverbs 13:22

One night in our apartment I watched my daughter Amber and my son J eat two plates of food each. Amber said, "Ma, I miss this rice. This food is good." J's response was "Ma, no offense, but you should get fired more often. I like your home-cooked food." Wow, kids say the darnedest things. I had to laugh at that myself. J said that my getting fired from the Car Dealership was the best thing that could have happened because now my kids eat home-cooked meals and get to see me when they come home from school.

You know, sitting at home writing this book has brought back so many memories—some I would love to have forgotten forever, but it's been such a wake-up call for me. I have worked hard and lived a Christian life every day. I try to be the same way every time you see me regardless of how I feel at the time. When I was growing up I watched my mother work hard to give me the kind of life she didn't have. There wasn't a style of clothing or a pair of shoes that came in fashion that I didn't have, and the one thing she always did was share her time with me. Even if there was a party going on—like I said, our house was the weekend hangout—she always had time for me before her friends came over.

From Proverbs 13:22, I wanted to give my children such a fabulous life because they have gone through every trial I have gone through. My kids are some tough, strong little cookies. I love them so much, but when it came time for forgiveness, I had to ask them to forgive me for missing the family Thanksgiving in New York, I had to ask them to forgive me for missing Christmas and New Year's in New York, and I had to ask them to forgive me for missing the school field trips. The biggest forgiveness I had to ask was for having such poor money management. You see, I had what Joyce Meyers calls an approval addiction. I helped everyone so much, to the point where I gave my last and didn't realize I had placed myself and my kids back into a time of struggle. I prayed on it and lifted it up to God, and he dropped a new look on life in my spirit.

I can continue to work hard because a good man leaves an inheritance for his children's children, but now I have to share with my children—while God blesses us with life, I have to share life with them. I realized they like nice things, but they also like simple things. It can be something as simple as a home-cooked meal, or to sit and spend time with their mother. I am so grateful for my children. They are all like little adults. They can communicate with me and let me know the importance of family. God has humbled me, and I thank you, Lord, and just want to let you know "I get it." You all will have an "I get it" moment, and you will feel the same joy that I have in my heart. Through God's power to do the impossible, when he feels the time is fit he blesses me. "I get it." God and family will always come first. I have to prepare for my grandchildren, I have to continue to speak of God's goodness each and every day, I will continue to be a help to others, but God, "I get it."

I was giving what God blessed me with away to people that most likely should not have been blessed. So God humbled me, and I am grateful for the lesson he's taught me. I have to prove to God that I can handle the right-now blessing so that he will release the bigger blessings he has in store for my life.

Thank you, Lord.

Chapter 40

Amby

～

My youngest daughter, Amber, was such an active handful when she was younger. She was the one child that you couldn't go to the movie theater with because she would be crawling under the seats and trying to run up and down the aisles; you could just forget about trying to sit and enjoy the movie.

She also had an early interest in hairdressing. This little girl used to wait until Britt and Tiff went to sleep and then cut their hair. We'd wake up and follow the trail of braids leading right to Amber's bed. It got so we had to hide every scissor in the house so the big sisters could keep their hair.

Amber was not afraid to speak up and ask questions when things didn't make sense to her. One day we went to Red Lobster and the place setting included a bread plate (which was empty, of course). Amber looked at that plate and then looked right up at the waiter and asked him, "Why did you give me this empty plate? What am I going to do with this?"

The little sister also took on the role of family protector. When Tiff fell off her bike and was crying, Amber took charge. She ran up to Tiff and said, "Who did it? Tell me, Tiff. Who did it? I'll get them!"

Once when we were at my mom's house, my cousin Kevin was bothering Amber and wouldn't stop even after she told him to leave her alone. Since words hadn't gotten the result she wanted, Amber then picked up a marble ashtray and threw it at Kevin. Thank God her aim wasn't perfect; that ashtray nearly hit his head.

Since then, Amber has grown into a very loving, sweet young lady. She doesn't run in the aisles at the movie theater anymore. In fact, now she dreams of going to film school to direct movies. I am in the process of sending her for a six-week course to get her started.

Chapter 41

Respect

For this book, I've been researching and speaking to my relatives about my life. I got on my knees and prayed to God to give me what he wanted me to write. I prayed that someone, even if it is just one woman, can take something away from my story that just might help them get a fresh start in life. I told him, "God, you have watched over me so much, and so many times you allowed me another chance...." I have to tell everything now. I am exposing myself so that you can see the glory of God in my life.

I am sitting here a single mother of four beautiful children. My oldest children's father was labeled a drug kingpin in Virginia. He would always tell me that if I ever left him he would kill me and bury me where no one would find me. Imagine someone standing in your face saying those words. Imagine you're young. I was barely in my twenties, so while he was telling me this I actually was taking it lightly. I didn't realize the severity of what he was telling me. God covered me, he protected me. Just from my association with Anthony I could have been locked up or gotten into something I had no clue about. Thank you, Jesus.

My two younger kids' dad Duke has decided he does not want to pay $550 a month in child support anymore. He has never taken any interest in calling the kids or even trying to see them; however, when his brother made an attempt at that, my ex acted such a fool that the kids said they did not want to go visit their cousin in Georgia anymore. One time he spoke with Amber on the phone when she was at her sister Shavonna's house in New York. Amber told him, "You don't call us or buy us anything. You didn't even send us a toy for Christmas," and he told Amber that I was the one who wouldn't let him see them. What he doesn't realize is that I would never badmouth him to my kids because I don't want to be the bad guy. My kids know me though, so his act didn't work with

Amber. Another time Tiff was home and her sister called my house and then put him on the phone. Tiff said that when he told Amber "it's your father" she said, "No, you are not; my mother is my father and my mother."

On the contrary to what Duke may think, I never badmouth him to the children at all; he's done bad in their eyes all by himself. Amber recently came to me and said, "Mom, I am changing my name to carry your last name." She said she uses Craft in school whenever she does schoolwork. I explained to her that is not her legal name and that she could not do that. She said, "I do not want to carry his name anymore and when I get old enough I will change it." This came up in connection with my youngest daughter's dream of becoming a minority female movie director. Amber will be attending film making school and she knows the course is very expensive, so she decided she wanted to ask her dad to help her mother pay for it. I first told her not to call him and ask, only because I didn't want her to get her heart broken and become disappointed. But she insisted on calling to ask him, and of course he would not help. I knew he wouldn't. I let her call because I was not going to be the bad guy in this. I let her experience it herself so that although she already knew he cared only for himself she didn't think I would ever stop her from attempting to reach out to him. It broke my heart. Even knowing how he would respond, I was still hoping for the positive.

Not that Duke has given me much reason to hope that he will change and start caring for his children. See, he's been trying to get his child support order lowered from $550 a month, but in truth I have not even been receiving that much. He is over $25,000 in arrears. I guess he feels he should have more money than his own children. Last week I received a weekly check of $24. For all of the previous month I received only $460, and the month before that only $452. Whatever amount I do receive I divide in two and let Amber and Jesurun purchase whatever they may need for that month. Well, when I told Amber I just received $23.89 to split she became very excited and said maybe he finally will change and help out. She thought I was saying $2,389. I had to correct her and tell her the true amount on the check, and her next response was "Wow, I guess that means that's all I'm worth to him." I told her no worries, whatever they need I will get it for them as usual.

Let me reiterate some things: First, he is only supposed to pay $550 per month that was ordered for one child back in 1998. (I decided never to go back to court to get an increase by adding Jesurun because he didn't even want to pay the order for just Amber.) Second, he is over $25,000 in arrears because I never received anything from him for years until the child support office finally caught up with him; and third, he's not even paying the full amount of the child support order. So, parents, I know that if I can raise four children as a single parent with the two oldest already in college, then as hard as it may be, you can do it too. I go back and forth when I get frustrated and I think about getting a lawyer and suing him for the child support arrearage; I get mad that he just does not give a damn and just does not want to support his children, all while he's living with a woman that has five children, none of which are his. I pray at times that he was in the state of Maryland so that he could be locked up for nonpayment of his child support. But in the end I just place my feelings and frustrations into God's hands, because until Duke does right by all of his children he will never have anything.

Ladies, it disturbs me when I see a man trying to take care of his children but because he went on with his life you don't want to let him see the kids. I sit here as a single parent and watch my kids' father make no attempt to be in their lives. I am there for everything. I am a football fan and a boxing fan; everyone knows I'm Floyd Mayweather's number one fan. I used to take J to the Washington Redskins games every week. When he was on the football team, his sisters and I would be there every week rooting him on. We even had customized jerseys with his number on them. Mine said "J-Rod's mom" and the girls' said "J-Rod's sisters." He told me one day, "Ma, you know more about football than some of the dads. You should be a team coach." What I am trying to say is that the children are very important; it's not about the adults. I am a single parent, but my child is not going to see me stressing out about it. I will be there for everything; I don't care if I have to get in the mud and get dirty. I am determined that if my children feel like something is missing it will not be because of Mommy.

Parents, please carry yourself in a way that your children will respect you.

Chapter 42

Faith

Do not settle or be discouraged. Get ready for God's blessing. Stay in faith; you are in a good position of new level, new growth. God knows what you are capable of. If he hadn't taken away my job at the Car Dealership, I would never have had the time to write this book. God knew, and he will never close one door without opening another.

I decided that today was going to be the start of my new beginning. You will see it in my attitude; I will walk with the boldness of God all over me. I know that God is with me and he will never leave nor forsake me. I will stay prayed up, I will stay in my word, and I will continue to walk towards the promises that God has shown me. Right now my bank account is in the negative and I don't know how I will be able to pay my rent next month because when God said move he shoved me out the door. I will walk by faith and not by sight. It is very, very important that you understand my circumstances, because when I blossom I want you to know it is God and only God that has made it come to pass.

One day back in 2006, a lady walked up to me in the dealership I was working in and asked if I was the owner. I told her no, I was the finance director. I'll never forget her next words. "For now," she said. "But someday God will give you a dealership that you will own." Then, just a couple of months later, someone else spoke those same prophetic words over me. Since then, I've known that someday I will own a dealership, and I will run it with integrity. This is now coming to pass. It is part of my blossoming. I have been looking at dealership locations, small ones, but I haven't understood why it was so difficult to pick one up, especially with so many locations closing down. But after hearing Joel Osteen's message about being pruned to blossom, I have realized what the problem is. See, I've been thinking small, but when God blesses me it will be big so that he can get the glory.

This year I was in the middle of a bankruptcy, I have no money in the bank, I lost my job and am not receiving unemployment, I have one daughter starting college and another in her last year of college, my ex-husband is trying to get his child support lowered once again because he feels he deserves to have more than his children. Right now I have bills due without a clue how they will get paid, and I am driving my daughter's car, a 2002 Kia Sephia with 92,000 miles and a cracked windshield. Not long ago we moved from a four-bedroom, four-bath townhome to a two-bedroom, one-bath apartment on the third floor of a walkup building, and I am so grateful to God just to have a roof over our heads.

I want to make all of this clear and lay it out for you because when my situation changes it will be all because of God and I want all the praise to go to him. You will see what God can do. God is giving me a dealership of my own, one where I can continue to serve his people honestly and with the utmost integrity. Keep in mind that right now I cannot even afford the business plan; I had one made and I am on a payment plan to pay for it. I am standing on his word over my life. Thank you, Pastor Joel Osteen, for the right-now word. I receive it. From this day forward, just sit back and watch as God creates the greatest opportunity out of what was meant to harm me. I will go city to city to spread his word and show that God is the only one that can do the impossible. Increase is coming forth. My setback was just a setup for a comeback. I will continue to walk by faith and not by sight. Thank you, Jesus.

Behold, I will do a new thing,
Now it shall spring forth;
Shall you not know it?
I will even make a road in the wilderness
And rivers in the desert.
Isaiah 43:19

Chapter 43

Meeting the Honorable Dr. Cornel West

Just a week or so after receiving that message from Joel Osteen, I had the opportunity of being at the Radio One station headquarters for a meet-and-greet with Dr. Cornel West. It was such an honor and another historical day for me. Ten to twelve community leaders were invited, and we all talked amongst ourselves as we waited for Dr. West to complete his live on-air interview.

When the door opened all you could see was Dr. West's smile—yes, that gap in the tooth lit up the room like a fluorescent light. He glided in so gracefully and he was so very humble, very soft-spoken but with strong words. He was an instant inspiration to all of us. Dr. West went around the room personally shaking hands with each individual and getting our names. When he was getting close to me all I could say was "Glory to God. Thank you, Jesus, for the favor you are allowing me." Despite all the challenges I'd been going through in the past months, despite the turmoil, change and uncertainty, I was still being given these moments of great opportunity and promise. This was another reminder to me to stay on my path towards my blessed future.

Dr. West shook my hand and with a smile on his face he did a gentleman's bow and said, "My sister, it is good to meet you." I told him it was an honor for me and I appreciated all he has done for my generation to look up to. He then gave me a hug and I was frozen, absolutely couldn't move. You see, I wasn't just some groupie meeting a celebrity. This man was a part of history. He was a Black Panther. He was in the stories I listened to growing up. Dr. West was a recovering cancer patient, and he just reminded me so much of my grandpa—very strong spoken but the sweetest person you could meet.

The weather that day was cold, in the forties, it was raining out and my hair was wet, but it was all worth it since I had the pleasure of meeting Dr. Cornel West. I would gladly do it again.

Chapter 44

The Twins, My Brothers Craig and Greg

As I wrote a little earlier in the book, I was not raised in a house with my brothers. They were raised a few blocks away by their paternal grandmother. I want to tell them I love them and I am very proud of the two of them. My brothers and I refused to be a product of our environment. I never once saw my brothers sell drugs. Just as with my father, their father was not around. My mother was young and immature when they were born, but God was so amazing—he covered them and placed them with a woman that in the end turned them into good men.

They are by no means perfect—we are all human, no one in the world is perfect—but they didn't use their situation as a handicap. They didn't go out and rob people, sell poison drugs to people, and they definitely never physically harmed anyone. I am writing this for you. You two have somehow turned me into the big little sister. I appreciate how much you guys respect me and how much you value my opinions. So when I received the call from my aunt Ann and my brother Craig that my brother Bubba needed my help in December 2009, that was the very first time in a long time that no matter what I had going on, nothing was going to stop me from getting home to New York.

Gregory (Bubba), when you were going through your trials, not one of our family members was going to give up on you, no one knew how to tolerate it anymore. They tell me that when you hear my voice on the phone, even though I'm all the way in Maryland, your demeanor changes and you go from cussing everyone out to a quiet man within a matter of seconds. And when the kids and I came up just to see you and for that entire weekend you didn't go into a drunken state, my sweet dear loving brother, that gave me all the hope that I knew you could get that monkey off your back. I know the road is going to be hard, but as I write these words with tears in my eyes, you have me and Craig forever. We will ride that ride with you, and I am here for you. I will continue to pray for you every night for God to take the taste for alcohol away from you. Brother, remember we witnessed God deliver our mother so she could walk away and never touch drugs again. He did it for her (for our family), and surely he can do it for you. When you say to me "I love you, Sis" and I say "I love you more," trust that I mean it wholeheartedly. Those words I would never take lightly, and as my kids have taught me I will never hold them in again.

Craig (or as everyone calls you, Weenie), I used to worry about you so much because although you are a hardworking man you scared me when I saw you take on the ways of our uncle. Women, women, and more women. I sat at my nephew James's birthday party next to his mother and watched you and your girlfriend parade around with just your and your girlfriend's friends, all while T didn't know anyone at the party and thought your girlfriend was just James's godmother. You know what I did, I told T, "Go get your son," because I was not going to sit and watch that happen to her. I pulled you aside and told you many years ago to get your s*** together because you were wrong. Of course instantly your girlfriend at the time did not like me, and I was not saved then so I could care less. But you hurt my feelings, not because you ended up marrying that very woman and cheating on her as well, but because I just found out that I had a two-year-old nephew I never even saw a picture of. When I spoke to Aunt Ann and she told me you come around a lot and do not bring the baby, I told her to invite you to bring him, what you have done as an adult has nothing to do with him—he is family and will be treated as such. However, again I had no idea he was nearly two years old; I thought he was just a few months old.

I really feel bad that you repeated this cycle. Generational curses are being broken off our family, the women are no longer on welfare, in the younger generation both your nieces have gone to college, so I'm praying to God that the curse will be broken off you and you will become a father and learn how to be a better man. Again I pray the same for myself, that when I get married I will know how to be a wife pleasing to God. Don't let your sons see you dog their mothers. I do not want them to treat women the very same way, or even worse, they might come to resent you. Your sister, your aunts, and even your mother raised kids alone. Please don't do that to your children's mother.

I have been noticing such a change in you I can say I am proud of. Keep God first in your life. My children told me once about myself, "You are acting like your father." That was the very same thing I never wanted to be. I love you very, very much, Big Brother, and I will love you even more when I see you become a role model for your sons. You know I laughed at you when I saw you chasing a toddler around and changing diapers. Don't mind me—keep up the good work in trying to walk in the right direction. I'm breaking my cycle of being in unequally yoked relationships, and I will continue to pray for the generational curse to be broken off you.

I love you both. I'm so proud that I am your sister. Don't worry—we know change is not an overnight thing. Just keep it up.

Chapter 45

Ready to Bloom

It's December 2009, time to switch and walk into my new season. However, I cannot start 2010 until I thank God for bringing me from May 1970 through this very hour. One song that touches my heart—the song that I have to shout and do a dance on, the one song that sends chills through my body, that fits perfectly for this book, that makes me yell hallelujah and thank God with tears coming down my face, down on bended knee—is Walter Hawkins and Yvette Flunder singing "Thank You Lord (for all you've done for me)." Thank you, Mr. Hawkins, for a song for a time such as this.

I'm sure 2010 will be another momentous year for me. Most people have songs they like. I've picked out my two songs for the year. They're both by Bishop Paul S. Morton of Full Gospel Baptist Church Fellowship: "Don't Do It Without Me" and "Let It Rain."

I did win my unemployment appeal, so I've had some money coming in. The owners of the Car Dealership didn't even bother to show up to the appeal hearing. (Once again, God was right on time!) There was enough money to allow me to get ahead on rent, so I don't have to worry about that right now. I've set up a corporation already and am working on getting ready to pursue my dealer's license. A few years ago, two different people spoke prophetic words to me, telling me I would one day own a car dealership. Well, their prophecy is about to come to pass. It took some time. It took going through that mess at the Car Dealership and being humbled and taken down to my core. But that was all a part of God's plan. You see, I first had to be pruned so that I could blossom, and now that blossom is beginning to open. I have no doubt that I will soon be the owner of a luxury car dealership that will offer people their dream cars, but more importantly, this will be a business where the customer will be treated fairly and honestly. I know this will come to pass because when God places a vision on your heart, he will also provide the provisions.

This goal received a major boost on December 10, an amazing day that I will mark on my calendar. I was asked to come out to an event called The Community Investment & Economic Empowerment Forum 2009. This was an event filled with elite players in our community: Dr. Lonise Bias, Dr. E. Faye Williams, Esq., First Lady of Prince George's County Leslie E. Johnson, Pastor Anthony Maclin, Barbara Stanford, Deputy Chief Administrative Officer of Prince George's County David Byrd, and Mark Oliver, director of small business for the U.S. Department of the Interior. When these people learned of my dream of owning my very own luxury car dealership, they told me to bring it to Prince George's County. Here I am sitting in the midst of all of these great men and women and they are telling me, "Oh no, you are not looking in Anne Arundel County. You need to come to PG County."

We all had to stand and introduce ourselves. Ironically, my turn came right after Dr. Bias, just as at the First Ladies Awards. I said, "Hi. My name is Shanise Craft. You may have heard me on the *Matt Anderson Show* on 104.1 FM, where Askshanise sponsored 'That's my story and I'm sticking to it.' I have been in the car business for about fifteen years, with hopes of owning my own luxury car dealership. I am a single mother of four children. My oldest finishes college on December 16. I have one that is a freshman in college and two who are college bound, and I just finished writing a book on my life story." The entire room applauded. First Lady Johnson said to me, "Your story should be a movie." Wow, she prophetically spoke that word over my story. I sat at the table with these awesome men and women who more importantly are men and women of God. They took an interest in me and said they would connect me to the right people to help bring the dealership to the PG County area.

Meanwhile, my surprising new career as a motivational speaker continues to develop. Who would have thought that my life could ever offer inspiration to anyone? I never got to walk across the stage at my high school graduation because I was busy being a young single parent involved in a controlling relationship with a drug dealer. Later I went through marriage and then divorce, only to end up as a single parent once again. I struggled to feed my kids and get them to school while we all lived in one hotel room after my own father kicked us out of his house. Did I realize at the time that I was going through these things for a reason? If I did, I surely never thought the reason would be so I could bring inspiration to other single parents. But that is what I'm doing, and that is what I will continue to do, because that is the path God has set me on. Many people think God cannot use them. I stand in awe and total amazement for all that he has brought me through. All I can say is "Thank you, Lord, for seeing fit to use me to help spread your word through my testimony and speak of your goodness!"

I believe God brought me to the point where I am today because he wanted to get my attention. I have been through a few bad relationships, have given away most of my money buying men huge gifts, watches, cars, and motorcycles because I was not equally yoked with them in the first place and didn't want them to feel bad that I had more than they had (bad choice). I didn't invest in the proper things, like houses. Instead I used my money to buy furs, jewelry, cars—all depreciating assets—and I ended up left with nothing. God has humbled me, and I am so grateful to God for doing so because now when he blesses me I will know exactly how to take care of what he allows me to have.

I've shared my story with many audiences, from the First Ladies Awards to Fox 5 DC. I've been honored with an award from the National Congress of Black Women. I spoke at a very special foster-care event that featured celebrities like Mike Winans Jr. and Darryl "DMC" McDaniels. I've been asked to make several more appearances, and I even had to turn one down recently so I could take a weekend to visit family in New York. You see, I may be branching out and preparing to blossom, but at the same time I'm also reaching back to my roots. This is important. Your roots ground you and provide nourishment, while God's light brings you new energy and shows you the direction you should grow in. Without both God's love and the strong roots of family, your branches will wither and your blossoms will never open.

Everything you have just read is the story of my roots. Soon the world will see the beauty of my blossoming. You've seen where I've been now watch what I'm about to become!

At the First Ladies Awards. *Photos by Gerald Evans Photography.*

Shanise at the First Ladies Awards.

First Ladies Awards honorees. Left to right: Dr. Lonise Bias of The Len and Jay Bias Foundation; Denise Rolarke Barnes, publisher of the *Washington Informer*; Edura Govan, executive director of International Business Kids; Dr. Charlene Dukes, president of Prince George's Community College; Shanise Craft; Cynthia Brazelton, pastor at Victory Christian Ministries International; Sheila Stewart; Leslie E. Johnson, first lady of Prince George's County; Singer Mya's sister; Edith M. Johnson, pastor at Miracle Temple P.H.C.; Trina Jenkins; Nichole Thomas, community activist and wife of Washington Wizards center Etan Thomas.

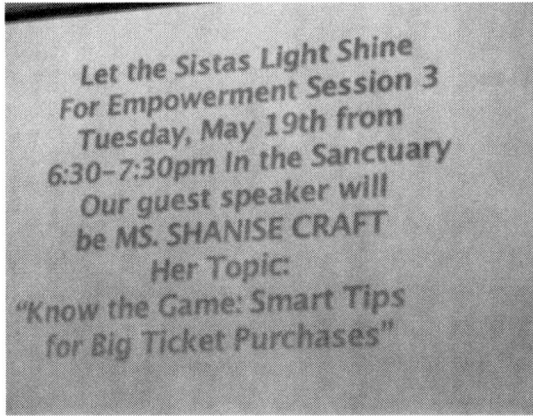

Screen from Empowerment Temple Church.

Speaking at Empowerment Temple Church.

National Congress of Black Women Awards Ceremony, 2009. Left to right, Peter Harvey, Regina Kelly, Shanise Craft, Dr. E. Faye Williams, Esq., Kimberly Anyadike, Janet Langhart Cohen, Judge Denise Langford Morris.

Meeting the Honorable Dr. Cornel West.

New Year's Eve 2009. Front: Deasia (Nunu), Jas, Sade (Fufu). Middle: Mom, Aunt Ann, Monique (Nikki). Back: Aunt Valerie, Sheka.

All five kids: Britt, Shavonna, Tiff, Amber, and Jesurun.

Ephesian – 6-12 wrestle against principal
Isiah   14 satan plan to take over Heaven.

Breinigsville, PA USA
21 June 2010

240335BV00004B/5/P

9 781616 588120